ASEAN-EU Partnership

The Untold Story

ASEAN-EU Partnership

The Untold Story

Editors

Tommy Koh
Ambassador-at-Large, Singapore

Yeo Lay Hwee
European Union Centre, Singapore

 **World Scientific**

NEW JERSEY · LONDON · SINGAPORE · BEIJING · SHANGHAI · HONG KONG · TAIPEI · CHENNAI · TOKYO

Published by

World Scientific Publishing Co. Pte. Ltd.

5 Toh Tuck Link, Singapore 596224

USA office: 27 Warren Street, Suite 401-402, Hackensack, NJ 07601

UK office: 57 Shelton Street, Covent Garden, London WC2H 9HE

Library of Congress Cataloging-in-Publication Data
Names: Koh, Tommy T. B. (Tommy Thong Bee), 1937– editor. | Yeo, Lay Hwee, editor.
Title: ASEAN-EU partnership : the untold story / editors, Tommy Koh, Lay Hwee Yeo.
Description: First edition. | Singapore ; Hackensack, NJ : World Scientific, 2020. |
  Includes bibliographical references and index.
Identifiers: LCCN 2020037063 | ISBN 9789811223105 (hardcover) |
  ISBN 9789811224225 (paperback) | ISBN 9789811223112 (ebook)
Subjects: LCSH: Southeast Asia--Foreign relations--European Union countries. |
  European Union countries--Foreign relations--Southeast Asia. | ASEAN. | European Union.
Classification: LCC DS525.8 .A74 2020 | DDC 341.242/20959--dc23
LC record available at https://lccn.loc.gov/2020037063

British Library Cataloguing-in-Publication Data
A catalogue record for this book is available from the British Library.

Copyright © 2020 by World Scientific Publishing Co. Pte. Ltd.

All rights reserved. This book, or parts thereof, may not be reproduced in any form or by any means, electronic or mechanical, including photocopying, recording or any information storage and retrieval system now known or to be invented, without written permission from the publisher.

For photocopying of material in this volume, please pay a copying fee through the Copyright Clearance Center, Inc., 222 Rosewood Drive, Danvers, MA 01923, USA. In this case permission to photocopy is not required from the publisher.

For any available supplementary material, please visit
https://www.worldscientific.com/worldscibooks/10.1142/11905#t=suppl

Foreword

The Association of Southeast Asian Nations (ASEAN) and the European Union (EU) are often regarded as two of the more successful regional organisations in the world. Ties between ASEAN and the EU date back to 1972, when the European Economic Community became the first external party to establish relations with ASEAN. Linkages between Europe and Southeast Asia go back even further. Yet the story of the multifaceted relationship between the EU and ASEAN and its member states has seldom been told and not always sufficiently appreciated. I thank the two editors of the book, Tommy Koh and Yeo Lay Hwee, for their timely initiative. This publication is particularly welcome during the period when Singapore serves as ASEAN's coordinator for ASEAN-EU Dialogue Relations.

I am heartened that Tommy and Lay Hwee have managed to gather essays by writers from all ten ASEAN Member States. Southeast Asia is a region known for its diversity, and these varied views undoubtably contribute to a deeper understanding of the rich array of ASEAN-EU cooperation. It is also important that the book addresses our commonalities as well as differences. Given our unique political, economic, and socio-cultural contexts, there will understandably be issues on which ASEAN and the EU hold divergent perspectives. Notably, these do not come in the way of the spirit of cooperation that underpins ASEAN-EU ties.

It is important that ASEAN and the EU continue building on our historical relationship to explore more that we could do together. I am glad that this book highlights this.

In particular, the ASEAN-EU Free Trade Agreement and ASEAN-EU Comprehensive Air Transport Agreement will bring tangible benefits to our people, and it is my hope that both will be concluded soon. Looking further ahead, I can see both sides doing more together in cyber security and smart cities. Published in the wake of the Coronavirus Disease 2019 (COVID-19) pandemic, the book also underscores the need for both regions to deepen our collaboration as we confront the pandemic and its aftermath.

The ideas contained in these essays are particularly salient at a time when proponents of regional integration and globalisation are contending with rising nationalism and protectionism. ASEAN and the EU cannot lay claim to the secrets of successful integration. Nevertheless, I hope that this book will serve as valuable food for thought for officials, scholars, students and members of the public as we look to grasp opportunities and confront the challenges that face our two regions.

Dr Vivian Balakrishnan
Minister for Foreign Affairs, Singapore

Contents

Foreword v

About the Contributors xi

Part One
Our Engagement and Cooperation

1. ASEAN and EU: From Donor-Recipient
   Relations to Partnership with a Strategic Purpose 3
   Yeo Lay Hwee

2. ASEAN-EU Economic Relations: A Shared Present
   and Future 13
   Pushpanathan Sundram

3. Political and Security Cooperation Between
   ASEAN and the EU 27
   V. P. Hirubalan

Part Two
Our Similarities and Differences

4. ASEAN and EU: Similarities and Differences 37
   Tommy Koh

5. A Few Things That ASEAN Has Outdone the EU 43
   Termsak Chalermpalanupap

6. Human Rights in the ASEAN-EU Relationship:
   Finding Common Ground 49
   Shashi Jayakumar

7. Convergence and Divergence:
   ASEAN's and the EU's Responses to the Rohingya Crisis 57
   Noeleen Heyzer and Lilianne Fan

Part Three
Diverse and Evolving Bilateral Ties

8. Brunei Darussalam-European Union Relations:
   Moving Beyond Diplomatic Niceties 65
   Osman Patra

9. Cambodia-EU Relations: Beyond Everything-but-Arms 75
   Chheang Vannarith

10. Indonesia-EU Relations: Close Partners or
    Distant Associates? 85
    Evi Fitriani

11. Laos-EU Relations: A Laos Perspective 91
    Sayakane Sisouvong

12. Malaysia-EU Relations: Themes and Evolution 101
    Nur Shahadah Jamil

13. Myanmar, ASEAN and EU: Finding the Nexus 111
    Moe Thuzar

14. Navigating the Nadir of Philippines-European Union
    Relations 121
    Sol Iglesias

15. The Perception-Expectations Gap:
    Recalibrating Singapore-EU Relations 137
    Yeo Lay Hwee

16. Thailand-EU Ties: A Toxic Love Affair 145
    Kavi Chongkittavorn

17. Vietnam-EU Relations: A Success Story 149
    Hoang Thi Ha

Part Four
Enhanced Cooperation into the Future

18. The ASEAN-EU Comprehensive Air Transport
    Agreement (CATA): Potential and Reality 161
    Alan Khee-Jin Tan

19. The European Union and ASEAN:
    Deepening Cooperation in Human Security 169
    Mely Caballero-Anthony

20. ASEAN-EU Trade Talks: Friends in Need 179
    Jaya Ratnam

Index 185

About the Contributors

Dr Yeo Lay Hwee is Director of the European Union Centre, Nanyang Technological University. She is also Council Secretary at the Singapore Institute of International Affairs, Adjunct Fellow at the S. Rajaratnam School of International Studies and Adjunct Faculty at the Singapore Management University.

Mr Pushpanathan Sundram was the Deputy Secretary General of ASEAN from 2009 to 2011. He held various senior positions in the ASEAN Secretariat as a professional staff from 1997 to 2008. He is currently the CEO of PublicPolicyAsia Advisors Pte Ltd, a business advisory firm in Singapore.

Mr V. P. Hirubalan is a former Singaporean diplomat who served in Jakarta, Brunei, Saudi Arabia, and the Philippines. He last served as Deputy Secretary General in the ASEAN Secretariat, in charge of the Political and Security Department before retiring from public service.

Professor Tommy Koh is Ambassador-at-large at the Singapore's Ministry of Foreign Affairs. He is also Chairman of the Centre for International Law and Rector of Tembusu College, National University of Singapore. Professor Koh was the founding Executive Director of the Asia-Europe Foundation.

Dr Termsak Chalermpalanupap is a Visiting Fellow at the Thailand Studies Programme of the ISEAS-Yusof Ishak Institute. He was previously Researcher at the Institute's ASEAN Studies Centre. Before joining the Institute in July 2012, he had served nearly 20 years at the ASEAN Secretariat, where his last post was Director for ASEAN Political and Security Cooperation.

Dr Shashi Jayakumar is Head of the Centre of Excellence for National Security (CENS), at the S. Rajaratnam School of International Studies, Nanyang Technological University. Since 2019 he has also been Singapore's representative to the ASEAN Intergovernmental Commission on Human Rights (AICHR).

Dr Noeleen Heyzer is a member of the UN Secretary General's High Level Advisory Board on Mediation. She was an Under-Secretary-General of the United Nations (2007–2015) and the first woman to serve as the Executive Secretary of the UN Economic and Social Commission for Asia and the Pacific.

Ms Lilianne Fan is International Director and Co-Founder of Geutanyoë Foundation, a regional humanitarian organisation based in Kuala Lumpur, Malaysia and Aceh, Indonesia; Regional Director of Rohingya Project; and Chair of the Asia Pacific Refugee Rights Network's Rohingya Working Group.

Pengiran Dato Paduka Osman Patra currently serves as CEO and Director of a number of companies in Brunei Darussalam, namely, Kehasan Waste to Energy Management Centre; Freme Travel Agency; and Oriental Sawmill Company. He retired as Permanent Secretary of the Ministry of Foreign Affairs and Trade of Brunei Darussalam in January 2012, a position he held since 2002.

Dr Chheang Vannarith is President of the Asian Vision Institute (AVI), an independent think tank based in Phnom Penh. His research interests focus on geopolitics and international political economy of Southeast Asia.

Dr Evi Fitriani is Associate Professor of International Relations and Head of Miriam Budiardjo Resource Center (MBRC) at the Faculty of Social and Political Sciences, Universitas Indonesia (FISIP UI). She is also co-founder of European Studies Programme of Universitas Indonesia and ASEAN Studies Center of FISIP UI.

Ambassador Sayakane Sisouvong is a career diplomat, and was the first Lao citizen to serve as Deputy Secretary General of ASEAN. He had served at the Permanent Mission of Lao to the UN and as Lao Ambassador to the United Kingdom, and was Permanent Secretary of Ministry of Foreign Affairs before his retirement. After 35 years serving Lao Government, Ambassador Sisouvong is now a free-lance advisor to several business groups and companies, including the East-West Consultancy Ltd, based in the United Kingdom.

Dr Nur Shahadah Jamil is a research fellow at the East Asian International Relations (EAIR) Caucus in Malaysia. She is also an associate member of Institute of China Studies, University of Malaya (UM) and currently serving the Malaysian Anti-Corruption Commission (MACC) as special officer to MACC's Deputy Chief Commissioner (Prevention).

Ms Moe Thuzar is a Fellow at the ISEAS-Yusof Ishak Institute in Singapore. Formerly a lead researcher at the ASEAN Studies Centre at ISEAS, she is currently co-coordinator of the ISEAS' Myanmar Studies Programme. Moe has served at the ASEAN Secretariat and in the Myanmar Foreign Service prior to joining ISEAS. She is researching Burma's Cold War foreign policy for her PhD dissertation.

Dr Sol Iglesias was the first female, first Asian Director of Intellectual Exchange at the Asia-Europe Foundation. She has a Ph.D. in Southeast Asian Studies and a M.A. in Political

Science from the National University of Singapore as well as a M.A. in International Affairs from the Fletcher School of Law and Diplomacy at Tufts University and a B.A. in Public Administration from the University of the Philippines.

Mr Kavi Chongkittavorn is a senior fellow at the Institute of Security and International Studies, Chulalongkorn University.

Ms Hoang Thi Ha is Lead Researcher (Political & Security Affairs) at the ASEAN Studies Centre, ISEAS-Yusof Ishak Institute.

Dr Alan Khee-Jin Tan is Professor of Aviation Law at the National University of Singapore Faculty of Law. He is Asia's leading aviation law academic and was a Hauser Global Visiting Professor at New York University. He has done consultancy work for ASEAN, the governments of Sri Lanka and Indonesia and airlines including AirAsia, Cebu Pacific and Royal Brunei.

Dr Mely Caballero-Anthony is Professor of International Relations and Head of the Centre for Non-Traditional Security (NTS) Studies at the S. Rajaratnam School of International Studies (RSIS), Nanyang Technological University, Singapore. Prof. Anthony's research interests include regionalism and multilateralism in Asia-Pacific, human security and non-traditional security, conflict prevention and global governance

Ambassador Jaya Ratnam is Singapore's Ambassador to Belgium concurrently accredited to the European Union as well as the Netherlands and Luxembourg. Mr Ratnam has served in various postings including to Malaysia, Indonesia, UN (Geneva) and prior to his current appointment in Belgium, he was Singapore's High Commissioner to Brunei.

Part One

Our Engagement and Cooperation

1

ASEAN AND EU

From Donor-Recipient Relations to Partnership with a Strategic Purpose

Yeo Lay Hwee

Introduction

The European Union (EU) is one of ASEAN's oldest dialogue partners. While economic ties between the two blocs have progressed steadily, and diplomatic and political relations have broadened, ASEAN's cooperation with the EU has not reached its full potential. This is in part because of the different perceptions and approaches to issues such as human rights, the use of sanctions and the sustainability agenda, compounded by misunderstanding accentuated by the very different institutional structures and priorities of the two regional organisations. The latter often lead to a certain degree of exasperation and hence, after more than 40 years, the desire to raise the partnership to a strategic level remained on hold. This chapter will provide a historical overview into the trials and tribulations of the ASEAN-EU partnership from 1972 to 2020.

From ASEAN-EC to ASEAN-EU Relations

Relations between the Association of Southeast Asian Nations (ASEAN) and the European Union (EU) (then the European Community), which date back to 1972, constitute one of the oldest group-to-group relationships. Concern about the implications of the UK joining the European Community (EC) — UK was then a key trading partner for several ASEAN members — ASEAN initiated the informal dialogue aimed at achieving greater market access for ASEAN's exports and a price stabilization scheme for ASEAN's primary commodities. ASEAN launched a Special Coordination Committee to conduct regular dialogue with the EC. This later became the ASEAN-Brussels Committee (ABC) comprising ASEAN ambassadors accredited to the EC.

The EC became one of ASEAN's official dialogue partners in 1977. The inaugural ASEAN-EC Ministerial Meeting (AEMM) in 1978 gave ASEAN-EC relations a boost and accorded the relations a greater political significance.

During the 2nd AEMM in Kuala Lumpur in 1980, the ASEAN-EC Cooperation Agreement was signed providing the legal and institutional framework to develop further the inter-regional ties. The main emphasis of the Agreement was on economic cooperation and development, extending the Most Favoured Nation (MFN) treatment to the contracting parties. However, despite this Agreement, ASEAN until the 1980s remained at the bottom of the EC's hierarchy of relations, below even that of the African, Caribbean and Pacific (ACP) and Latin American countries.

Throughout the 1980s, two issues dominated the political dialogue — Afghanistan and Cambodia (then Kampuchea).

This rather low-key relationship went into an acrimonious phase over democracy and human rights issues in the early 1990s with the end of the Cold War. The Treaty of Maastricht signed in 1991 transformed the European Community to the European Union, reflecting the aspirations of the EU not only to be an economic power but a political actor with its own Common Foreign and Security Policy (CFSP). One of the objectives of EU's CFSP as contained in the Maastricht Treaty was to develop and consolidate democracy, rule of law and respect for human rights.

In the 1994 EU's New Asia Strategy, the EU acknowledged the longstanding relationship that it had with ASEAN and saw EU-ASEAN relations as a cornerstone of its dialogue with the broader Asian region. This more pragmatic turn to capitalize on the EU-ASEAN partnership for broader economic gains was reflected in the 11th AEMM held in Karlsruhe in September 1994. The issue over unrest in East Timor in the early 1990s and the concerns over human rights abuse by the Indonesian army in East Timor was sidestepped and dropped from the agenda of the bloc-to-bloc meeting. Instead, Portugal — the former colonial ruler of East Timor — had a separate discussion of the conditions in East Timor with Indonesia. An EU-ASEAN Eminent Persons Group (EPG) was commissioned to develop a vision of EU-ASEAN relations towards the year 2000 and beyond.

Unfortunately, the recommendations in both the 1996 EPG Report on "A Strategy for a New Partnership" and the Commission's own Communication to the Council and European Parliament in July 1996 on "Creating a new dynamic in EU-ASEAN Relations" on revitalizing the EU-ASEAN ties did not have a chance to be translated into concrete measures. A series of events and number of factors, notably the Asian Financial Crisis, the launch of what the EU seen as another inter-regional platform for cooperation, the Asia-Europe Meeting (ASEM) process, and the potential enlargement of ASEAN to include Cambodia, Laos and Myanmar changed the dynamics and further impacted the EU-ASEAN relations. In particular, Myanmar's entry into ASEAN in 1997 brought new tensions and strains to the EU-ASEAN dialogue. Myanmar was branded by the EU as a rogue state with terrible human rights record, and with the EU which has one of its objectives as promoting democracy, human rights and rule of law in its CFSP, Myanmar became a constant irritant in EU-ASEAN relations.

The events of 9/11 and international terrorism, the dramatic rise of China and the "re-invention" of ASEAN in the aftermath of the Asian Financial Crisis led the EU to reassess its relations with ASEAN and its member states. The Commission's policy paper in 2003 entitled "A new partnership with Southeast Asia" recommended that the EU adopt a pragmatic approach towards ASEAN and its member states, and forge relations at both bilateral and inter-regional level. In this paper, the EU acknowledged that the EU-ASEAN partnership should not be held hostage by Myanmar. There were strong reasons for EU to enhance its relations with ASEAN, including first and foremost, the fight against international terrorism, as well as the underlying economic imperatives. ASEAN was also in the process of rethinking its regional cooperation model and seeking greater institutionalization as it contemplated moving towards the building of an ASEAN Community. The latter move was warmly welcomed by the EU who had long purveyed its own regional integration as a model that could be useful for other regions.

From 2003 the EU scaled up efforts to engage ASEAN in particular in the area of providing support for capacity building towards integration with programmes such as the ASEAN Programme for Regional Integration Support (APRIS) from 2003–2010 to the current ASEAN Regional Integration Support from the EU (ARISE). The EU also stepped up cooperation in counter-terrorism with several ASEAN member states such as Indonesia, in the wake of the Bali bombing and other terrorist attacks.

In its 2006 Global Europe strategy, ASEAN was also identified as one of the priority region for EU's trade and investments. This led the EU to try to pursue an ambitious bloc-to-bloc Free Trade Agreement (FTA) with ASEAN. EU-ASEAN FTA negotiations were launched in 2007. After six rounds, the negotiations were suspended in 2009 when the EU realized how differently

ASEAN function and the great disparities in institutional capacities and developmental models. The insurmountable differences plus the ongoing disputes with Myanmar over its human rights record forced the EU to abandon the ambitious inter-regional FTA in favour of bilateral FTAs with individual ASEAN member states.

Despite such efforts, EU-ASEAN relations continued to be plagued by disagreement over developments in Myanmar and how to engage the country, with ASEAN preferring constructive engagement to the EU's imposition of sanctions. It was not until Myanmar's election in 2011 that set in motion a credible reform process, and a number of other reasons that finally led the EU to pursue in earnest a comprehensive partnership with ASEAN with strategic purpose.

What are some of these reasons? First, the US pivot (or rebalancing) to Asia in 2011 changed the geopolitical undercurrents in the Asia-Pacific region. The contest between the US and China in Southeast Asia, rising tensions in the South China Sea, made this region an important test case of how China will reshape Asian security and regional governance. Second, ASEAN's efforts to build an ASEAN Economic Community with a market of over 600 million consumers were making some progress. Despite the low ambitions of the ASEAN Economic Community with the key objectives of creating a single production base, and efforts to transform ASEAN into an attractive investment destination, Southeast Asia's generally good growth trajectory provides opportunities for the EU in search of new growth areas to aid its economic recovery. Taken as a single entity, ASEAN is EU's 3rd largest trading partner outside of Europe, after US and China. ASEAN was also the fifth most important location of EU foreign direct investments abroad in 2014, with €184 billion in FDI stocks.[1]

---

[1] Yeo Lay Hwee, "ASEAN-EU Dialogue — Moving Towards Strategic Relevance", in *50 Years of ASEAN and Singapore*, edited by Tommy Koh, Chang Li Lin and Sharon Seah, 2015.

In May 2015, the EU issued a Joint Communication on its relations with ASEAN entitled "The EU and ASEAN: A Partnership with a Strategic Purpose". In this Communication, the EU acknowledged that "it has a strategic interest in strengthening its relationship with the Association of Southeast Asian Nations because "ASEAN is at the heart of the efforts to build a more robust regional security order in the wider Asia-Pacific".[2]

EU-ASEAN Relations with a Strategic Purpose?

The EU's pivot towards Asia following Obama's moves was in part a reflection of the central reality of the growing economic importance of the Asian region to the EU's continued prosperity. This growing importance also comes with the realization that the EU can no longer ignore the increasing geopolitical tensions and potential security risks that could upset the growth trajectory in the region. The "old Asia strategy" of the 1990s, which focused primarily on the economic opportunities, is no longer tenable. The EU accepted the centrality of ASEAN in the security of the region, and made concerted efforts to renew and enhance the long-standing partnership.

The EU and ASEAN are two most successful regional organisations. Both have played an important role in the peace and stability of their respective regions. They have remained resilient and relevant in confronting various crises. They can therefore do more together to not only support each other's role in their respective regions, but also potentially contribute to global peace and stability.

The external environment that the EU and ASEAN operate in has also changed drastically. The rising tensions and rivalry between the US and China have created volatility and uncertainties that need to be managed to ensure that overall peace and

---

[2] Joint Communication to the European Parliament and the Council, The EU and ASEAN: A partnership with a strategic purpose (Brussels, 18 August 2015), p. 2.

development is not derailed. The Covid-19 global pandemic has exacerbated the Sino-US tensions and accelerated existing trends of economic nationalism and de-globalisation disrupting global supply chains and the connectivity conundrum.

How will the heightened tensions and strategic rivalry impact geopolitics and would the EU and ASEAN be forced to choose between the US and China? How to manage the rising protectionist sentiments and continue to support rules-based multilateral approach towards economic exchange? What norms and principles should guide our cooperation? All these are questions that both the EU an ASEAN and their respective member states need to be actively engaged in to prevent further chaos and disruptions, and to address the common challenges facing us.

All these common challenges should create the dynamics for the EU and ASEAN to upgrade their partnership to one with a strategic purpose. Both have reasons to strengthen regional governance and build bridges across regions to forge a partnership that can support peace and development. Instead of simply accepting, the move towards a multipolar world based on power and spheres of influence, both should work to support a multilateral order based on interests, rules and norms. Instead of relying on the US hegemonic leadership (which in any case is eroding), the two regional organisations could work towards a system of issues-based functional leadership.

A truly strategic partnership between the EU and ASEAN could be better realised if both regional organisations could get their act together to become strategic actors in their own right. ASEAN need to do more to shore up its centrality and remain in the driving seat of regional architectures, and the EU need to do more to achieve strategic autonomy. For these to happen, ASEAN has to be more institutionalised, and the EU need to become more flexible and pragmatic. In addition, both need to become more coherent and cohesive but also more agile.

In a complex, highly contested and ambiguous world, the EU need to become more flexible. The increasing divergences within the EU meant that it is often unable to reach quick consensus or act resolutely. Hence, the EU while continuing its efforts to strengthen its unity must also allow for more flexible "coalition of the willing" constellation in its policy. Such "coalition of the willing" arrangements must be embedded in trust and solidarity and within a coherent strategic outlook.

For ASEAN, the exact opposite is necessary. ASEAN's current modus operandi does not privilege collective actions over individual efforts. Its inter-governmental structure and strict interpretation of sovereign equality often results in joint political declarations but not necessarily common actions. ASEAN is sensitively attuned to the divergent interests of its member states and take a pragmatic approach to respect individual member states' interests. This is sometimes done at the expense of collective regional interests exposing ASEAN to the dangers of being divided and weakened. ASEAN need to become more integrated to be a more effective regional organisation that can navigate and withstand the current rising tensions between China and the US, and deal with increased protectionism. It must speak more with one voice and undertake more joint actions. Reconciling intra-ASEAN differences deserves greater attention..

Both regional organisations were founded on the desire for peace and stability. While borne of the Cold War era, they have managed to adapt to the changes in the external environment and stay relevant. ASEAN and EU have to strengthen their efforts to remain relevant. To do so, they should step up their diplomatic and pragmatic engagements with each other and leverage each other's respective strengths to shape a new emerging order that is more inclusive.

They can strengthen their engagement at different levels:

- Between EU member states and ASEAN member states;
- Through more ambitious inter-regional EU-ASEAN endeavours; and
- Through joint EU-ASEAN efforts in multilateral forums and institutions such as the ASEAN Regional Forum (ARF), the Asia-Europe Meeting (ASEM), United Nations, etc.

At the multilateral level, there are two areas that both can work on. This is first, in the area of connectivity in the ASEM agenda, and second, to come together whether in WTO, UN to shape general principles and norms to govern emerging areas of cooperation and challenges such as the digital economy, artificial intelligence, etc.

Other more specific recommendations on how we can navigate our differences and move towards a strategic partnership are:

First, avoiding the "singularity trap" — do not allow one single issue to derail the broader strategic need for engagement. For example, issue over palm oil should be resolved between those ASEAN member states and EU separately. It has long been ASEAN way not to allow bilateral issues (even those between ASEAN) to impact broader regional interests.

Second, having a certain level of maturity to deal with differences — just as we expect the EU to respect the "ASEAN way", ASEAN should also respect the "EU's norms". Where the two collide, the approach is to agree to disagree and continue to seek convergence on issues of common interest.

Before we can have a strategic partnership of substance, both the EU and ASEAN must show their commitment through "sustained presence" in each other's region. The EU has real presence in ASEAN now with its various programmes to build capacity in the ASEAN Secretariat, and various bilateral development projects with individual ASEAN member states. However, the EU still suffers from low visibility and hence need to do more at the level of public diplomacy.

For ASEAN, there is a need for more concerted effort to display ASEAN and engage the different EU institutions (such as the European Parliament) in Brussels. As the EU and its member states are proud of their democratic principles, ASEAN must also be more aware and conscious of the lobbying by other actors, and be open to engage European civil society, NGOs and businesses.

In summary, there is much potential to elevate the long-standing ASEAN-EU relations to a strategic partnership. What is needed is the political will and willingness to look beyond some of the thorny issues and focus on the bigger strategic landscape, and find pragmatic and practical ways forward. As the EU and ASEAN stepped up in their roles to coordinate and support their respective member states in the fight against Covid-19 and dealing with the economic consequences, an inter-regional platform to exchange information and facilitate policy learning and coordination should also be mounted. As tensions further rise between the US and China over the pandemic, both the EU and ASEAN need to work with other like-minded partners to prevent a new cold war becoming hot.

2

ASEAN-EU Economic Relations
A Shared Present and Future

Pushpanathan Sundram

Introduction: The Origins

Relations between the Association of Southeast Asian Nations (ASEAN) and the European Union (EU) are now about five decades old. Informal ties were established in 1972. In 1977 the European Economic Community (the forerunner to the EU) became one of ASEAN's first formal dialogue partner. In the years since, the relationship has evolved across many dimensions.

The EU originated with the European Coal and Steel Community in 1952, an economically integrated common market with regulated industrial production and prices for coal and steel. By 1957 decisions were taken to deepen economic integration resulting in the European Economic Community with goals of removing internal trade barriers to create a common market and establishing common external trade policy. Membership now encompasses almost all of Western Europe and much of Central and Eastern Europe.

ASEAN enjoyed a similar path of development. From its inception in 1967, the region has taken strides towards economic cooperation. A key milestone in 1992 was the creation of the ASEAN Free Trade Area (AFTA), which comprised the then six ASEAN members — Brunei, Indonesia, Malaysia, the Philippines, Singapore and Thailand. These efforts were advanced with the more sophisticated ASEAN Investment Area (AIA), ratified in 1998. Similarly, ASEAN enlarged to encompass all of Southeast Asia with Vietnam joining in 1995, Lao PDR and Myanmar (1997), and Cambodia (1999). The journey has continued with the establishment of the ASEAN Economic Community (AEC) in 2015 and the realisation of bilateral free trade agreements between ASEAN and China, Japan, South Korea, India and Australia and New Zealand by 2015. The work on the realisation of the Single Market under the AEC continues with the implementation of the AEC Blueprint 2025.[1]

Leading trading blocs

Today, the EU and ASEAN are premier trading blocs. The EU is the world's largest single market, the biggest importer and exporter, and the leading investor and recipient of foreign direct investment (FDI). Although economic growth is presently anaemic, and even with Brexit, with 445 million consumers, it remains the second largest economy globally after the US. The EU's transparent rules and regulations and secure legal framework create a stable and attractive environment for investors worldwide.

ASEAN is the world's fifth largest economy with a dynamic market of over 640 million consumers.[2] In the global economic slowdown following the Global Financial Crisis, ASEAN has remained one of the bright spots for global growth — bolstered by an increasingly affluent middle class and a well-educated population. ASEAN is expected to be the fourth largest economy by 2030 after US, EU and China.

---

[1] The AEC Blueprint 2025 builds on the AEC 2015 blueprint, and seeks the realisation of a) a highly integrated and cohesive economy; b) a competitive, innovative and dynamic ASEAN; c) enhanced connectivity and sectoral cooperation; d) a resilient, inclusive, people-oriented and people-centred ASEAN; and e) a global ASEAN.
[2] The ASEAN Secretariat. *ASEAN Integration Report 2019*. October 2019. Available online at https://asean.org/storage/2019/11/ASEAN-integration-report-2019.pdf

The establishment of the AEC in 2015 added to the economic dynamism, as the region moves towards a globally competitive single market. According to the ASEAN Secretariat, the "AEC is the realisation of the region's end goal of economic integration".[3] The AEC is envisioned as a single market and production base. Its successful realisation also provides a boost to ASEAN-EU relations as it establishes ASEAN's commitment to freer movement of capital and skilled labour, and the harmonisation in trade and investment laws. All of these make doing business with ASEAN as a region substantially easier and a lot more attractive.

Evolution of the Economic Relationship Between ASEAN and EU

ASEAN reached out to the EEC in 1972. Through the mid-1970s, both regions maintained informal dialogue aimed at market access for ASEAN's exports and price stabilisation for its primary commodities. In the late 1970s, relations strengthened when the EC sought to establish a regional presence. Both partners also sought to capitalise on the economic integration achieved in their respective regions. But the value of merchandise trade remained small — in 1978, for instance, total ASEAN exports to the EC stood at ECU4.2 billion, while the EC's exports to ASEAN stood marginally lower at ECU3.9 billion.[4]

The 1980 ASEAN-EC Cooperation Agreement, concluded two years later, was a key milestone supporting trade and economic ties. It emphasised economic cooperation and extended the "Most Favoured Nation" status, where the best trade terms were given to contracting parties. The Cooperation Agreement

---

[3] The ASEAN Secretariat. *About AEC*. Available online at http://investasean.asean.org/index.php/page/view/asean-economic-community/view/670/newsid/755/about-aec.html

[4] European Commission. *3rd EC/ ASEAN Business Council Meeting*. 20 October 1987. Available online at https://ec.europa.eu/commission/presscorner/detail/en/memo_87_100. ECU stands for European Currency Unit. In 1978, 1 ECU was equal to USD1.2.

laid the foundations for an economic partnership, paving the way for greater integration.

Trade and investment trends over the past 50 years

At the beginning of the 1970s, both regions were experiencing relatively strong growth, albeit from different starting points. Trade relations for ASEAN countries centred on securing greater market access to European markets for primary commodities and textiles. For these states who were still emerging from colonialism, new markets were key for growth and development. For Europe, new markets provided an opportunity to sustain their unprecedented growth levels. Trade increased almost ten-fold between 1971 and 1979, and European investments into the region overtook American and Japanese investments.[5]

Following the economic crisis of the late 1970s, there was a global shift towards trade liberalisation. Increases in trade volumes continued throughout the 1980s, tripling by 1991. During the 1980s, manufactured products as a percentage of total traded goods rose from 23.8% to 60%.[6] During this period, both regions' economies witnessed substantial structural changes. In Europe, manufacturing entered relative decline, and economic output increasingly focused on the service sector. This was related to structural changes in the ASEAN region, where economies gained in sophistication. Manufacturing, often offshored from Europe, increased in importance in ASEAN. ASEAN textiles exports as a percentage of the total rose from 4% in 1975 to 14% in 1993, while export of raw materials decreased from 36% to 13%.[7] By 1988, total ASEAN merchandise exports to the

---

[5] Center for European Integration Studies. *ASEAN and the European Union: A Bumpy Interregional Relationship.* 2001. Available online at https://core.ac.uk/download/pdf/5073913.pdf

[6] Ibid.

[7] European Commission. *EC-ASEAN Relations.* 23 July 1993. Available online at https://ec.europa.eu/commission/presscorner/detail/en/MEMO_93_32

EC stood at ECU12.2 billion, while total EC exports to ASEAN stood at ECU10.7 billion.[8]

Despite this, as of 1989, ASEAN's share of the EC's trade amounted to only 3.1% with the EC's share of ASEAN trade sat higher at 15%. Europe, during this time, prioritised the Americas as trading partners.[9]

Notwithstanding further economic liberalisation with the collapse of Communism, relations waned during the 1990s. Barriers emerged over human rights and democracy, particularly regarding East Timor and Myanmar. Priorities for the EC changed. The eastern enlargement of the EC and the completion of the European Single Market diverted trade—and focus—away from ASEAN. ASEAN's efforts, too, were focused elsewhere. The group had already joined the EU's Generalised Scheme of Preferences. Other attractions included removing import duties from developing countries, and FTAs with other regional groupings and large economies. The multitude of opportunities for trade development meant ASEAN-EU relations played second fiddle for both regions.

In 1997, ASEAN countries were hit by the Asian Financial Crisis that resulted in a rapid contraction of their economies and a substantial outflow of capital from the region. The crisis also led to political transition in several ASEAN countries, and especially Indonesia. It also brought an increased focus on economic governance, which until then had not been that much of a priority for the ASEAN economies. The consequences of these positive changes meant that the region became better aligned for cooperation with Europe.

Come the early 2000s, ASEAN-EU relations began to improve. The EU's approach to ASEAN became more

---

[8] European Commission. *EEC/ ASEAN Relations*. 15 February 1990. Available online at https://ec.europa.eu/commission/presscorner/detail/en/memo_90_8

[9] Center for European Integration Studies. *ASEAN and the European Union: A Bumpy Interregional Relationship*. 2001. Available online at https://core.ac.uk/download/pdf/5073913.pdf

pragmatic and ASEAN's move towards greater institutionalisation also helped. But significantly, the impressive post-crisis rebound of the ASEAN economies meant that the importance of good economic ties grew in relative significance to the liberal ideals of the EU. The expansion of an affluent young middle class created a seductive consumer base for European exports. Furthermore, the US pivot to Asia pressured the EU to remain competitive. These resulted in the 2003 Trans-Regional EU-ASEAN Trade Initiative, which proposed improvements to trade, and the 2006 formal prioritisation of ASEAN for trade and investments by the EU.

The economic relationship between the two groupings has been consistently strong in recent years. Merchandise trade reached €236.7 billion in 2018, a remarkable increase from the €139.9 billion worth of merchandise trade between them in 2008.[10] Manufactured goods dominated trade both ways, hovering around 83–87% for EU exports to ASEAN and 78–85% for ASEAN exports to EU between 2008 and 2018.[11] Over the same period, trade in services almost tripled, rising from €29.9 billion in 2005 to €85.5 billion in 2017. The relationship's strength is unsurprising as it is economically complementary. The EU has a very strong service sector, whereas ASEAN's strength is in manufactured exports.

Investment ties between the two groupings have improved over the past few years too. Between 2000 and 2018, the EU has provided about one-fifth of all FDI coming into ASEAN. In 2018, the EU was the largest external source of FDI, with inflows into

---

[10] Eurostat. *ASEAN-EU — international trade in goods statistics*. Available online at https://ec.europa.eu/eurostat/statistics-explained/index.php/ASEAN-EU_-_international_trade_in_goods_statistics

[11] Eurostat. *Manufactured goods dominate trade with ASEAN partners*. 7 November 2019. Available online at https://ec.europa.eu/eurostat/statistics-explained/index.php/ASEAN-EU_-_international_trade_in_goods_statistics#Manufactured_goods_dominate_trade_with_ASEAN_partners

ASEAN totalling $22 billion.[12] While on an upward trend, investment has been volatile due to the 2002 and 2012 global slowdowns and the 2008–09 Global Financial Crisis. Manufacturing dominated investments between 2005 and 2010, but in recent years this has shifted towards finance and insurance activities.

The inflow of capital from EU to ASEAN is expected to continue on the expectation that ASEAN's economic growth will continue outpacing the growth in other large economies globally. Strong economic growth in the region is resulting in a growing middle class that is increasingly affluent with significant disposable incomes.

Improving legal and regulatory frameworks will also play an important role in continuing to draw FDI from EU, as will the harmonisation of standards and deeper regional economic integration, which will allow investors to consider the ASEAN region as one economy as opposed to a grouping of 10 different markets. The implementation of the AEC in 2015 has been an important step in ASEAN, demonstrating its commitment to community building.

The ties binding these two regions go far beyond the desire for greater trade and investment flows. The EU is the largest donor to ASEAN, providing over €200 million in support to ASEAN regional integration and connectivity. In addition, the EU has provided over €2 billion in bilateral assistance to ASEAN member states. This is combined with other initiatives such as the EU nurturing ambitions of labour mobility and high-performance computing alongside cooperation in cybersecurity, aviation, sustainability and intelligent transport. The picture is clear — the EU sees the ASEAN region as an "EU in development" and as a natural partner. It is thus supporting a framework of development that parallels its own history in many

---

[12] The ASEAN Secretariat Jakarta. *ASEAN Investment Report 2019*. October 2019. Available online at http://investasean.asean.org/files/upload/Web%20InvestASEAN%20-%20AIR%202019.pdf

ways. Collaboration between the two trading blocs is ongoing at multiple levels and in a variety of sectors, and it is bringing the two regions' key economic stakeholders closer together. This will play an important role in how ASEAN-EU relations are shaped in the years to come.

The fruits of the ASEAN-EU cooperation are evident today. In 2018, the EU was ASEAN's second largest trading partner and ASEAN the EU's third. The trade balance is in favour of ASEAN, with the gap increasing since 2008.[13] In 2018, ASEAN exported over €140 billion to the EU, mainly in machinery and transport equipment, agricultural products, and textiles and clothing. The main imports from the EU to ASEAN are chemical products and machinery and transport equipment, totalling €97 billion. Separately, the EU is the largest investor in ASEAN with €337 billion of FDI stocks in 2017. Although not as large, ASEAN investment into Europe has been steadily rising too, reaching €141 billion in 2017.[14] All of these numbers are expected to continue increasing in the coming years.

Exports from ASEAN to the EU are currently concentrated in the Netherlands, the UK and Germany. The picture is more spread-out for ASEAN member states, with Singapore, Vietnam, Thailand, Malaysia, Indonesia and the Philippines accounting for 95% of ASEAN-EU trade in 2018.[15] The scale and importance of these economic ties are cemented, but forging a closer relationship has also been challenging.

---

[13] Eurostat. *ASEAN-EU - international trade in goods statistics*. September 2019. Available online at https://ec.europa.eu/eurostat/statistics-explained/index.php/ASEAN-EU_-_international_trade_in_goods_statistics

[14] European Commission. *Association of South East Asian Nations (ASEAN)*. 17 June 2019. Available online at https://ec.europa.eu/trade/policy/countries-and-regions/regions/asean/

[15] *EU struggles to strike trade pacts with major ASEAN countries*. Nikkei Asian Review. 4 August 2019. Available online at https://asia.nikkei.com/Politics/International-relations/EU-struggles-to-strike-trade-pacts-with-major-ASEAN-countries

Attempts at an ASEAN-EU FTA

A free trade agreement, whilst ambitious, is the pinnacle of economic integration and the next step in the ASEAN-EU relationship. Region-to-region trade agreement negotiations were launched in 2007. Despite positive assessments of feasibility, talks were suspended two years later. The barriers cited were ASEAN's lack of negotiating capacity and political will, difficulties in reaching collective positions, and diversities in economic structures across the ASEAN region. Even more significant for EU was Myanmar's human rights records. The EU's legal obligations towards universal human rights prevented progress and talks stalled.

With the regional FTA talks stalling, focus shifted to bilateral FTAs between the EU and individual ASEAN member states. In 2009, negotiations were launched with Singapore, Vietnam, Malaysia, Thailand, Indonesia and the Philippines. Trade agreement with Singapore came into effect in November 2019 and with Vietnam, the agreement was ratified in 2020 and will come into effect in August. Negotiations with Indonesia and the Philippines are ongoing but challenging; and negotiations with Malaysia and Thailand have stalled. Despite these challenges, the EU puts bilateral FTAs with individual ASEAN members high on their agenda. They view these agreements as stepping-stones towards a future FTA between the two blocs.

Interest towards a region-to-region FTA has been rekindled in 2016 in response to the changes both within ASEAN and in Europe, and also in the broader global context. Firstly, disparities across ASEAN economies had reduced. Perhaps more significantly, efforts of ASEAN economic integration had borne fruit with the ASEAN Economic Community (AEC). The hard-fought internal integration paved the way for international integration, with the region becoming a more significant single entity. Over the past decade, we have seen the formation of a less amorphous ASEAN identity, which has been the result of years of effort by member states and concerned stakeholders to bring 10 very different political and economic systems successfully under one umbrella.

The past few years have seen ASEAN liberalise its markets, moving against the global trend of increasing protectionism. This was perhaps helped by Singapore's economic success through a liberal economic model. Europe, on the other hand, was bruised by the Eurozone crisis, and Brexit, prompting re-engagement in negotiations. By March 2017, the EU and ASEAN agreed to relaunch negotiations and the 2018-2022 ASEAN-EU Plan of Action declared the parties' commitments to the FTA negotiations.

There should be no doubt that the future of the two regions lies in the successful culmination of a free trade agreement as that is in the best interests of both.

The Future of the ASEAN-EU Economic Relations

Successful FTA negotiations takes time with multifaceted challenges to address. In the case of ASEAN and EU, deals have only been struck with Singapore and Vietnam. On a region-to-region basis, issues preventing progress in 2007 continue to plague the partners today. The EU's view that bilateral trade pacts with individual member states are a stepping stone towards a region-region FTA, has not yet been successful. Conversely, these trade agreements have put the broader ASEAN-EU FTA on the backburner.

Coordinating positions among the consensus-based ASEAN member states remains tough. Significant challenges come from protecting domestic industries in some ASEAN member states from increased competition. Similarly, concerns exist over ability of ASEAN member states to make hard policy choices due to domestic politics. Additionally, Malaysia, the Philippines and Indonesia have been unwilling to embark on the expected liberalisation of their economies regarding procurement, competition and intellectual property rights.

Concerns go beyond the immediate economic impacts of trade. Negotiations with Indonesia and Malaysia ended over deforestation and sustainability issues after Brussels support the phasing out of palm oil imports to be used as biofuel for transport by 2030. Political and human rights challenges also threaten success — negotiations are stalled in Thailand over infringements to democracy, and the EU still has human rights concerns in Cambodia and Myanmar.

However, the huge expected gains from a region-to-region FTA push back against these challenges. An FTA is assumed to reduce the cost and complexity of trade. This will increase trade volume resulting in faster growth, and greater productivity and innovation, particularly for export-oriented sectors. The complementarity of the economic relationship also acts as a catalyst: the EU has much to gain from export of services and ASEAN for exports of goods. Europe also has geopolitical interests in promoting the region, particularly as it finds itself increasingly threatened by protectionism and unilateralism of the US.

For ASEAN, the benefits are multiple. There is the opportunity to diversify its economy. The adoption of the EU's higher standards will improve the quality of its exports to Europe and globally. Both these factors are crucial to a resilient and dynamic economy, an issue of grave importance given China's increasing economic prominence in the region. Financial investment also plays a huge role. China has deep pockets, and through the Belt and Road Initiative (BRI), it is steadily making inroads in a few of ASEAN region's economies. At one level, China's heavy investment in infrastructure augurs well for the less developed ASEAN economies. On the other hand, however, there are question marks around increased dependency on China and the strategic implications. The other key sources of inward FDI in ASEAN are the US and Japan, followed by South Korea.

Shifting global economic developments have reopened opportunities for closer ties. The US withdrawal from the Trans-Pacific Partnership (TPP), an agreement between 12 Asia-Pacific countries to liberalise trade in goods and services, is an opportunity for the EU to further extend relations into Southeast Asia. The vacuum left by the US may encourage ASEAN to place more emphasis on expanding trade relations with the EU, particularly as China's influence becomes more prevalent by the day.

Separately, the negotiations for the Regional Comprehensive Economic Partnership (RCEP) have ended with India existing. The RCEP is expected to be signed in 2020 by the remaining 15 countries (ASEAN-10 and China, Japan, South Korea, Australia and New Zealand). The long negotiation process for the RCEP could arguably help build ASEAN's capacity for the more challenging free trade talks with the EU. It is yet another step in what has been a steep learning process.

Finally, as the second largest economy in the EU, the impact of the UK's vote to leave the EU on ASEAN-EU relations remains to be seen. The UK has announced, at the end of 2019, its intention to deepen ties with ASEAN and to establish a dedicated UK Permanent Mission to ASEAN in Jakarta. Certainly, ASEAN will be keen to work towards closer economic ties with UK but it will certainly take time to mature.

The torchbearers for globalisation

After nearly 70 years of trade liberalisation, globalisation may be retreating. International economic cooperation is experiencing growing levels of resistance globally. Global merchandise trade volume growth is expected to fall to 2.6% in 2019, down from 3%

in 2017.[16] Protectionist trade measures are at a historical high with tensions continuing unabated. The US and China — the world's two largest economies — continue to tussle over tariffs and trade, impacting global supply chains adversely. Recent negotiations between US and China at the start of 2020 mark a step forward, but how the deal will be implemented remains a concern.

The backlash against globalisation is clearly having a strong impact. Brexit, election of Donald Trump, and the successes of nationalist parties in Europe (and elsewhere) all challenge openness, free trade and investment. It may be early days, but the growing anti-globalisation sentiment is a concern.

With the uncertainty in future of globalisation and free trade, ASEAN and the EU have an important role to play. As two of the world's largest economic groupings, they have an opportunity to push back against recent trends. Indeed, they are doing so. At a time when many are questioning multilateralism and retreating into economic nationalism, the EU and ASEAN remain bright spots backing globalisation. The two regions' economies have prospered as a result of a commitment to free trade, and there is no reason to expect this to change anytime soon.

Conclusion

ASEAN and the EU will remain committed to their respective regional integration and free trade. This commitment is driven by the belief that it is the most effective way of fostering stability and prosperity, advancing the international rules-based order and promoting fair and open markets within their respective regions. While there are undoubtedly challenges to entrenching

---

[16] World Trade Organization. *Global trade growth loses momentum as trade tensions persist.* 2 April 2019. Available online at https://www.wto.org/english/news_e/pres19_e/pr837_e.htm

the ASEAN-EU relationship further, how it pans out could define the future of globalisation and free trade and investment for the world. For these two regions, the relationship will remain strong given the complementarities in their economies and the huge potential ASEAN offers with its growing population and middle-income group. Similarly, as ASEAN economies expand and diversify, EU will continue to be a key market for exports. In essence, there is only one future for the two blocs, and it is one they share.

3

Political and Security Cooperation Between ASEAN and the EU

V. P. Hirubalan

ASEAN-EU relations span slightly more than four decades, and over the years has developed into a very beneficial and productive partnership. The EU is a major trading and investment partner for ASEAN and has contributed immensely to ASEAN's development, capacity building and integration efforts including narrowing the development gap among ASEAN Member States (AMS) and supporting ASEAN's community building. The EU has earmarked €200 million in development assistance for the period 2015-2023. The data and statistics show significant progress in ASEAN-EU relations in the economic and socio-cultural pillars with tangible benefits to both sides.

Cooperation in the political/security arena on the other hand, is more complicated. Each side has its own notion and perception of what political and security cooperation entails. The EU, which sees itself as a major power with global responsibilities, would like to play a greater role in this pillar and be placed on par with ASEAN's other dialogue partners such as the US, Russia, China and Japan. ASEAN on the other hand sees the present political/security cooperation level with the EU as about right. From ASEAN's perspective this is a relationship between two regional organisations, and in that regard must be different from ASEAN's dialogue relations with individual countries.

Existing Dialogue Mechanisms

The EU acceded to ASEAN's Treaty of Amity and Cooperation in 2012 which represented a political commitment to its relations with ASEAN. As with other Dialogue partners, ASEAN-EU political cooperation centres around a series of institutionalised meetings at various levels. ASEAN and EU do not have regular Summit level meetings, although it was recently agreed to convene ASEAN-EU Leaders Meeting in the side lines of the biennial ASEM (Asia Europe Meeting) Summits. Unlike ASEAN's other dialogue partnerships which is country-specific allowing all 10 ASEAN Leaders to meet with the leader of the dialogue partner, summit meetings with the EU is usually between ASEAN Leaders and the EU Council President. To commemorate the 40th Anniversary of ASEAN-EU relations in 2017, the Philippines as the then ASEAN Chair arranged for an ASEAN-EU Commemorative Summit with the EU represented by the then President of EU Council, Donald Tusk.

The two key mechanisms that manage ASEAN-EU political ties are the annual ASEAN-EU Post Ministerial Conference (PMC) held back to back with the ASEAN Foreign Ministers' Meeting (AMM), and the biennial ASEAN-EU Ministerial Meetings (AEMM) alternating between both regions. The EU High Representative for Foreign Affairs and Security Policy represents the EU at the annual PMC while the AEMM is a bigger meeting involving the Foreign Ministers from all members states of ASEAN and the EU. These two institutions frame and manage ASEAN-EU relations supported by the ASEAN-EU Senior Officials and an ASEAN-EU Joint Cooperative Council (JCC) based in Jakarta comprising ASEAN's Committee of Permanent Representatives and the EU Representative to ASEAN. The key document that presently governs relations between the two regional organisations is the ASEAN-EU Plan of Action (POA) 2018–2022, a road map of sorts to work towards an Enhanced Partnership. This POA has a comprehensive section on cooperation in the political and security pillar.

Security cooperation

The EU's security cooperation with ASEAN is quite substantial particularly in non-traditional security areas which includes transnational crime. The main channel for such cooperation is through a consultation mechanism with the ASEAN's Senior Officials Meeting on Transnational Crimes (SOMTC) covering areas such as counter-terrorism; money laundering; drug trafficking; arms smuggling; human trafficking; chemical, biological, radiological and nuclear (CBRN) risk mitigation; sea piracy and cybercrime. Institutional links between ASEANAPOL and EUROPOL were established in November 2016 as another channel to combat transnational crime. The EU has also extended support to ASEAN to develop a regional border management programme to enhance border security in the region. More recently, ASEAN and the EU have expanded cooperation to include maritime issues through an ASEAN-EU High Level Dialogue on Maritime Security Cooperation.

Beyond the formal mechanisms, the EU has shared its experiences by sponsoring capacity building programmes for officials from the ASEAN Secretariat and AMS in areas such as international maritime law, counter terrorism and cybercrime.

The other channel the EU uses to enhance security cooperation with ASEAN is through the ASEAN Regional Forum (ARF). Since 1998, the EU has co-hosted and co-chaired in partnership with ASEAN countries many ARF activities and workshops covering key areas such as disaster relief, counter-terrorism and transnational crimes, maritime security, small arms and light weapons and energy security. The EU's contribution has been especially noteworthy in trying to help the ARF evolve from a confidence building mechanism to promoting preventive diplomacy.

Lingering EU Unhappiness

There has been some unhappiness on the part of the EU over the lack of progress in three areas that it deems important for it to play its full potential in the ASEAN-EU Political and Security Pillar. This includes (i) the elevation of ASEAN-EU relations to a strategic partnership; (ii) membership in the East Asia Summit (EAS); and (iii) membership in the ASEAN Defense Ministers Meeting Plus (ADMM Plus).

The EU believes that as a major power it has a strategic role to play in the Southeast Asian region and wants ASEAN to accord it this status by elevating ASEAN-EU relations to the strategic level and including the EU as a full participant in the EAS and ADMM Plus. ASEAN has yet to come to any conclusion on whether the EU has the gravitas to play a strategic role in the region, and what value it can bring to the EAS and the ADMM Plus.

The issue is more complicated as some AMS have difficult relations with the EU over the latter's position on domestic policies and political developments in these countries. Although bilateral issues between the EU and individual AMS should theoretically not interfere with the broader ASEAN-EU relations, in reality those AMS which have difficult bilateral relations with the EU often do not support proposals that would enhance the EU's relationship with ASEAN in the political and security pillar.

Strategic partnership

The decision to work towards an ASEAN-EU strategic partnership was taken some 5 years ago at the 20th AEMM. EU officials frequently raise the subject both in formal and informal settings. However, ASEAN consensus on this issue is difficult to reach as those AMS who have problems in their bilateral relations with the EU opt to defer the decision.

At the 22nd AEMM held in Brussels in January 2019, it was agreed in principle to upgrade ASEAN-EU relations to a strategic partnership subject to details and timing to be worked out. The proviso on details and timing would suggest that granting the EU strategic partner status could be delayed until such time there is an ASEAN consensus on formalising the decision.

East Asia Summit

The EU has lobbied long and hard to have a seat in the EAS, believing that as a long standing and committed partner of ASEAN, and an organisation with global interests, it deserves to be made a member of this ASEAN-led Leaders' Level Strategic Dialogue. (Of ASEAN's ten dialogue partners, only the EU and Canada are not participants of this mechanism.) EU officials and ambassadors of EU countries based in Jakarta have regularly raised the subject of the EU's admission into the EAS arguing strongly that it has a strategic interest in the region and that it can add value to the process. Privately EU officials remarked that they could not understand why the EU was not included in the EAS whereas Russia was.

ASEAN has taken the position that the EAS, after the admission of the US and Russia in 2010, is at an optimal position and further expansion is not desirable. Initially, the EU believed that ASEAN was blocking EU's membership in the EAS. What it did not realise was that there was an understanding among the EAS members there was no need to expand the EAS. So even among the non-ASEAN EAS member there was agreement not to open the door. To ameliorate EU's unhappiness, ASEAN arranged for the EU Council President to participate in an EAS lunch in 2017 (being the 40th Anniversary of ASEAN-EU relations) together with other invited guests as a special one-off gesture. The EU still harbours the hope of eventually being included in the EAS.

ASEAN Defence Ministers Meeting Plus

In tandem with its desire to be a full partner in the EAS, the EU has also indicated its interest to actively contribute to the region's security and defence through participation in the ADMM Plus. ASEAN Defence officials are not certain how the EU as a regional organisation can contribute to this process. The EU does not have an armed forces as such. Informal consultations with the non-ASEAN participants of the ADMM Plus also reveal that none of them see the EU as being able to contribute actively to the ADMM Plus.

The EU has changed tack. In 2018, the ADMM Plus took a decision to allow non-ADMM Plus countries to participate as observers in ADMM Plus Expert Working Groups (EWG). These EWGs focus on specific areas of interest to further strengthen ADMM Plus cooperation and promote transparency and confidence building among the defence establishments of the participating countries. The EU has applied to participate as an observer in the EWG process probably in the hope that participation at this level could be a window to eventual membership in the ADMM Plus. However, as the present policy does not address the question of allowing regional organisations to participate as an observer, the EU request will only be addressed in 2020 – 2023 timeframe. The EU will probably not be pleased with this outcome.

Strengthening the Partnership

Moving forward, ASEAN and the EU must take into account the changing regional and global environments and adjust accordingly to ensure continued robust and effective cooperation. When Britain voted to leave the EU in 2016, in internal ASEAN discussions there was some worry over EU unity and resilience. In fact, it was not uncommon for Brexit to be cited in ASEAN meetings as a wake-up call for ASEAN's own integration and community-building efforts. Developments in the EU region over the past few years such as increasing nationalism, closing of borders, rise of protectionism and economic challenges, to name a few, and the potential impact of these on ASEAN-EU relations did raise concerns in ASEAN. However, candid discussions and exchange of views between ASEAN and the EU through existing mechanisms have proved useful in helping each organisation better understand developments and emerging challenges in each other's regions, and keep the relationship stable.

Overall, ASEAN-EU cooperation in the political and security pillar is deep and broad, and is likely to continue along its present trajectory. AMS have benefitted significantly from this cooperation, particularly in the non-traditional security sector. The EU has been generous in sharing experiences and arranging for capacity building programmes for ASEAN officials. The present political and security section of the ASEAN-EU POA 2018–2022 is a rich document that would bring cooperation in this pillar to a higher level if fully realised.

Steps should be taken to address the EU's lingering unhappiness in its cooperation with ASEAN in the political and security sector. The first move could be to enhance the partnership to the strategic level. This decision is completely within ASEAN's control unlike the EU's desire for membership in the EAS and ADMM Plus which would require the endorsement of all members of these mechanisms. It is interesting to note that in the ISEAS-Yusuf Ishak Institute's 2020 survey on the State of Southeast Asia, respondents tagged the EU as the entity in which they had the strongest confidence to provide leadership to maintain the rules-based order and uphold international law. The EU was also tagged as the second-most preferred and strategic partner for ASEAN, next to Japan, if ASEAN had to seek out third parties to hedge against the uncertainties of the US-China strategic rivalry. The respondents certainly had a positive view of the EU's potential as a strategic partner of ASEAN. ASEAN should take note of these sentiments and the changing geopolitical climate to strengthen its partnership with the EU.

Part Two

Our Similarities and Differences

4

ASEAN and EU
Similarities and Differences

Tommy Koh

The European Union is often referred to as the world's most successful regional organisation. In 2012, it won the Nobel Peace Prize, for keeping the peace in Europe for sixty years. ASEAN is often referred to as the second most successful regional organisation. In this essay, I would like to compare and contrast the similarities and differences between ASEAN and the EU. I will begin with the similarities.

Similarities

The first similarity is that both are regional organisations with legal personalities. The EU has 27 members and with a few more countries in Southeastern Europe knocking at its door. ASEAN has 10 members with Timor-Leste knocking on the door. I can think of no ASEAN member which is contemplating leaving the organisation.

The second similarity is that both were founded to promote peace. The EU was founded, after two disastrous world wars, to prevent the recurrence of war in Europe and to institutionalise peace through economic integration. ASEAN was founded to create a peaceful environment in Southeast Asia so that the ASEAN countries could focus their energies on their economic development.

The third similarity is that both seek to integrate the economies of their member states into a single market and production platform. In the case of the EU, there is freedom of movement of goods, services, capital and labour. In the case of ASEAN, the movement labour is not free. The ASEAN Charter only obliges the member states to facilitate the movement of business persons, professionals, talents and labour. This is a major difference between ASEAN and the EU. The free movement of persons in the EU became an emotional issue in the Brexit debate in 2016.

The fourth similarity is that both organisations share a commitment to human rights. The EU has a Charter of Fundamental Rights and ASEAN has a Declaration of Human Rights. The ASEAN Charter contains several provisions in its Preamble, Purposes and Principles, on human rights. ASEAN has two commissions on human rights:

(1) the ASEAN Intergovernmental Commission on Human Rights; and

(2) the Commission on the Rights of Women and Children. However, in the ASEAN charter, the focus of these Commissions is on the promotion of human rights leaving the protection of human rights to the respective national commissions. The EU has a Court of Justice of the European Union which can further act to protect the human rights of EU citizens specified under the Charter of Fundamental Right. It would be fair to say that the protection of human rights is stronger in the EU than in ASEAN.

The fifth similarity is that both ASEAN and the EU have concluded many free trade agreements or comprehensive economic partnership agreements with other countries. For example, the EU and Singapore have concluded a free trade agreement which came into effect on 21 November 2019. The

EU has concluded a similar agreement with Vietnam pending ratification. ASEAN has concluded such agreements with China, Japan, South Korea, India, Australia and New Zealand but not yet with the EU. The EU and ASEAN are currently studying the feasibility of negotiating such an agreement.

The sixth similarity is that both ASEAN and the EU hold regular political and economic dialogues with important external partners. The EU holds annual summits with its strategic partners such as the US, China, and Japan. ASEAN has created three forums to engage its external partners, namely, the ASEAN Regional Forum, ASEAN Plus Three and the East Asia Summit. In addition, ASEAN holds bilateral dialogues with its 10 Dialogue Partners. Finally, ASEAN holds an annual summit with the US, China, India, Japan and South Korea. Between ASEAN and EU, I think ASEAN has the stronger convening power. It is probably also due to the fact that Southeast Asia has become the region where all the major powers have an interest and where the competition between them for influence is the greatest.

Differences

There are several important differences between ASEAN and the EU. The first difference is that ASEAN is an intergovernmental organisation. The EU, in contrast, is a supranational organisation in which its member states have agreed, in certain areas, such as trade, to pool their sovereignties. In other words, the member states have voluntarily agreed to transfer their sovereignty to EU institutions in several policy areas. The pooled sovereignty is exercised by the EU institutions on behalf of the member states. This feature of the EU was probably one of the reasons for the British electorate to vote in favour of Brexit. They wanted to "take back control". British politicians succeeded in exploiting British nationalism against the EU.

The second difference is that the EU has a common currency called the euro. However, only 19 of the EU's 27 members are members of the Eurozone. ASEAN does not have a common currency and has no plans to do so. However, in the aftermath of the 1997 Asian Financial Crisis, ASEAN together with China, Japan and South Korea launched the so-called Chiang Mai Initiative. The project brings together the 13 Finance Ministers and Central Bank Governors. Their agenda is to promote greater financial cooperation among the 13 countries.

The third difference is that the EU has a Parliament and ASEAN does not. The European Parliament has the power to legislate as well as the power to veto budgets and appointments. ASEAN has the ASEAN Inter-Parliamentary Assembly which has only the power of moral suasion.

The fourth difference is that the EU has a very powerful Secretariat called the European Commission and ASEAN has a relatively small and weak Secretariat. The European Commission acts like a government and is entitled to enter into treaties. For example, the EU was allowed to sign and ratify the UN Convention on the Law of the Sea. The Commission has the power to put forward proposals for legislation. The ASEAN Charter has enhanced the power of the Secretary-General. One of his most important responsibilities is to issue an annual report card on each member state's compliance with its obligations. I am happy to say that the various ASEAN Secretaries-General have discharged this onerous responsibility with honesty and fairness.

The fifth difference is in the decision-making process. ASEAN takes all its decisions by consensus. The EU can decide by taking votes. There is a system of qualified majority voting requiring a double majority of 55% of member states and 65% of the EU population. However, in the area of common foreign and security policy, decisions are still based on unanimity. In ASEAN's case, there is an exception to the consensus rule: economic agreements can be adopted by a majority, using the

"ASEAN minus X" formula. The logic is that the majority can proceed first and the minority will catch up later.

The sixth difference is on language policy. The EU has 23 official languages. In the case of ASEAN, English is used as the sole medium for meetings and communications. This is an excellent example of ASEAN's pragmatism. The five non-English speaking countries, Cambodia, Indonesia, Laos, Thailand and Vietnam, were willing to use English and to learn to use English.

Conclusion

I want to conclude by expressing my confidence in the EU. I believe that the EU, without the UK, will be stronger and not weaker because it will be more cohesive. I do not believe that the EU will break up or that the euro will fail. There are, however, two emerging threats to the EU. The first is that, as time passes, fewer and fewer Europeans will remember horrors of the First and Second World Wars, which killed 37 million and 60 million people, respectively. They do not understand the importance of the European integration project. The second threat is posed by rising nationalism in several European countries. There is a trade-off between nationalism and European integration. In the same way, I believe that ASEAN will overcome its challenges and remain united and independent. Learning from the experience of the EU, ASEAN will redouble its efforts to ensure that it is not viewed as an elitist project. Instead, ASEAN must ensure that it enjoys the support of the 625 million citizens of ASEAN.

I have often been asked whether ASEAN will evolve to resemble the EU. My answer is that the EU is an inspiration but not a model for ASEAN. The histories, cultures and circumstances between the two regions are very different. ASEAN will, however, learn from the EU, both positive and negative lessons. In the end, ASEAN will determine its own destiny. It will develop its own model.

5

A Few Things That ASEAN Has Outdone the EU

Termsak Chalermpalanupap

Many of our friends in the EU may wonder why ASEAN cannot move faster in building its regional community, and create more concrete benefits for its own peoples. My quick answer is simply that ASEAN has greater political diversities, but very limited resources to act more decisively.

The political spectrum in ASEAN is mind-boggling. It includes authoritarian communist party rule in Laos and Vietnam, at one end, and the absolute monarchy in Brunei Darussalam, at the other end, with different shades of democracy in between the two extremes.

Since their ways and means of coming to government power greatly differ, political leaders in ASEAN states have developed different worldviews concerning the national interests which they have to defend. Defending national interests first is not always conducive to creating common regional interests in ASEAN. Hence, there is an existential need in ASEAN to make decisions cautiously by consultation and consensus. In practice, what eventually is agreed in the laborious ASEAN decision-making process is usually the least objectionable, but not always the most desirable ideas or things to do.

Unlike in the EU, ASEAN has no political criteria of membership. The main criterion for a prospective member to join

ASEAN is its geographical location, which must be in Southeast Asia. And of course there must be a consensus among all the existing members to support the admission of a new member.

In the EU, in order to qualify to apply for the EU membership, a European state must be a functioning multi-party democratic system with a good human rights protection regime, and a functioning market economy

ASEAN with a Shoestring Budget

Another important reason for the slow movement in ASEAN is the acute scarcity of resources. ASEAN has no source of revenue of its own. The budget for the annual operations of the ASEAN Secretariat in 2019 was only about US$20 million. Contribution to the budget is based on equal sharing—not by assessment of ability to contribute. The poorer members like Laos and Myanmar as well as the wealthier members like Singapore and Brunei Darussalam each contributed the same amount of US$2 million to fund the ASEAN Secretariat. ASEAN cost each of the 660 million people in ASEAN only 3 US cents per capita last year.

On the other hand, in 2019 the budget for the EU was about 165.8 billion euro, or about US$185.7 billion. Funding the EU cost each of the 513.5 million European citizens about US$362 per capita last year.

Therefore, in my opinion, comparing the EU with ASEAN is like comparing a world-class research university in Europe with a *kampong* primary school in Southeast Asia.

In spite of these disparities, ASEAN has actually outdone the EU in a few things. Perhaps the most significant of them all is the fact that none of its 10 members is contemplating quitting the Association of Southeast Asian Nations (ASEAN), as Professor Tommy Koh already mentioned in Chapter 4.

Moreover, ASEAN may soon expand its membership to embrace Timor-Leste into its fold. The youngest Southeast

Asian nation, which regained full independence in May 2002, has in March 2011, applied for ASEAN membership.[1]

ASEAN Still Benefits All Members

All member governments in ASEAN still see as valid the original reason for the establishment and the existence of ASEAN, i.e. to create and maintain regional peace and security, and to prevent the Balkanisation of Southeast Asia by external powers.

The peace-oriented principles, in the 1976 Treaty of Amity and Cooperation in Southeast Asia (TAC), and the Nuclear Weapon-Free Zone in Southeast Asia do benefit all ASEAN members. In the wake of the growing US-China rivalry, ASEAN provides its members with a safe collective choice of being "pro-ASEAN" without antagonising China or alienating the US.

Small members like Brunei Darussalam, Laos and Cambodia enjoy the sovereign equality in ASEAN that enhances their national security and independence. They also benefit from increased international recognition and support which comes with the ASEAN membership. Laos, for example, rejoiced in welcoming President Barack Obama who went to Vientiane for the ASEAN-US Summit and the East Asia Summit (EAS) in September 2016. If Laos were not the ASEAN Chairman and the host of the summits in 2016, the small land-locked country would probably not have an opportunity to welcome a US president to its land.

More economically developed members like Singapore, Malaysia, the Philippines, Thailand, and Vietnam take advantage of the growing economic opportunities of the ASEAN Economic Community (AEC) and ASEAN's external economic engagements with major trading partners. Indonesia,

---

[1] Timor-Leste's application has been under careful consideration in ASEAN. The main concern is whether Timor-Leste, with a population of only 1 million, will be able to participate fully in all ASEAN activities. A working group has been established by the ASEAN Coordinating Council (ACC) to assess Timor-Leste's preparation and readiness.

meanwhile, can still play a *de facto* leadership role of being the first among equals in ASEAN, like in leading ASEAN in the RCEP negotiations.

All in all every ASEAN member has something to gain from its participation in the Association.

Less Stress and Strain

No political leader of any ASEAN member government would ever dream of trying to gain any political advantage from calling a national referendum on the membership of his or her country in ASEAN. There has never been any discernible connection between popularity or disapproval of ASEAN and public opinion in any ASEAN country.

Another huge difference between ASEAN and the EU is that ASEAN agreements have seldom directly touched the life and livelihood of peoples in ASEAN countries

There is no "ASEAN citizenship" for peoples of ASEAN members to move around freely. Nationals of ASEAN countries do not have complete freedom of movement, or freedom of residency to live and work in other ASEAN countries. Nationals of ASEAN countries only enjoy visa-exemption when they visit other ASEAN countries as tourists.

In ASEAN, only Cambodia and the Philippines are parties to the 1951 UN Refugee Convention. The others in ASEAN do not have any legal obligation to receive refugees. Just a small number of Rohingya Muslims have entered Thailand, Malaysia, and Indonesia. ASEAN member countries in general do not face any stress and strain of intra-regional migration or influx of refugees the way the UK and several EU members have encountered in the past few years.

In the AEC there are efforts to facilitate movement of skilled labour. But recipient countries such as Singapore and Malaysia continue to maintain tight national control on migrant workers from all overseas sources. After nearly 10 years, discussions on a legal instrument for the protection of rights of migrant workers in ASEAN have little progress to show.

No Resentment Towards Jakarta

Another significant difference between ASEAN and the EU is the absence of any bureaucracy in ASEAN that could issue and impose legally binding regulations to inconvenience anyone in ASEAN. Commitments to ASEAN and implementation of ASEAN agreements are fulfilled under the implicit understanding of best national voluntary efforts with due consideration to unique national circumstances.

Not many in ASEAN know there is the ASEAN Secretariat in Jakarta (established in 1976). Fewer still know that the current Secretary-General of ASEAN (2018–2022) is Mr. Lim Jock Hoi from Brunei Darussalam.

Since little is known about ASEAN, the general public in each ASEAN country has thus no strong view about the ASEAN Secretariat in Jakarta one way or another; unlike in many EU member states where there is strong and vocal public resentment of the alleged arrogance of Eurocrats in the European Commission in Brussels.

Nevertheless, the growing number of ASEAN meetings and summits does create a financial strain on the poorer ASEAN member governments. One solution is to hold many of the routine meetings at the ASEAN Secretariat. The Indonesian Government has spent US$37 million in building new 16-storey twin towers to expand the premises of the ASEAN Secretariat, as part of its ambition of making Jakarta the "ASEAN capital" and "Brussels of the East".

Learning from the EU

During the drafting of the ASEAN Charter, members of the High Level Task Force on the Drafting of the ASEAN Charter undertook a working visit to Brussels in March 2007. They came back with two important lessons: Keeping the ASEAN Charter short and do not subject the draft ASEAN Charter to any referendum in ASEAN member states.

Consequently, the ASEAN Charter has only 55 articles and 4 annexes in 53 pages. The rejected European Constitution of 2004 had over 500 pages and numerous long annexes. Most of the voters in France and the Netherlands, who voted against it, never read the long document. They voted against it as a show of their disapproval of their governments at that time. If the draft ASEAN Charter were to be put to a referendum, the majority of voters in Myanmar would most likely reject it as a show of their disapproval of the ruling Myanmar junta in 2008.

Inside the ASEAN Charter, one can find the following "small achievements":

- One working language: ASEAN has agreed on using English as the (only) working language.
- One anthem: ASEAN has agreed on its anthem.[2]

When compared with the EU, ASEAN may be slow and modest. But we in ASEAN are proud of having ASEAN as it is moving forward into its 54th year of regional cooperation, doing what it can despite our great diversities and with limited resources.

We will continue to learn from the EU in order to develop ASEAN. We will work together in ASEAN, and cooperate with the EU and all external friends and partners, to build a successful ASEAN Community.

We in ASEAN intend to succeed, so that the world will have one fewer developing region to worry about.

---

[2] Subsequently, "The ASEAN Way" was adopted as the ASEAN anthem, following a region-wide contest in 2009. The winning entry came from three Thais: Mr. Kittikhun Sodprasert, Mr. Sampow Tri-udom, and Mrs. Prayom Valapatchra.

6

Human Rights in the ASEAN-EU Relationship
Finding Common Ground

Shashi Jayakumar

Institutions, systems of governance, and prisms through which human rights are viewed: all these things take a long time, centuries even, to develop. Europe had this time. The stability and coherent framework through which the EU views global issues is not something that developed overnight.

Time begets a certain uniformity. The EU has had various criteria before a state can accede to its ranks. Conditions are imposed, and behaviours expected in terms of respect for human rights for a nation to be accepted into the EU and EU bodies.

ASEAN did not — and does not — have this homogeneity. Its course of development proceeded very differently from the EU. ASEAN came together with a big bang, as it were, in 1967, with its founding nations being at different stages of economic developments, and having different political and legal systems. Some ASEAN Member States (AMS) did not have traditionally elected democratic governments (some at points in their history even had military coups).

Given these circumstances it would have been difficult for ASEAN in its initial decades to forge any sort of consensus on human rights — the issue was not a priority. Several AMS took the view that stability and security should be provided first, before human rights can be seen to. Various countries within ASEAN have their own approaches. Some have their own national human rights institutions (NHRIs) such as (Indonesia, Malaysia, Philippines and Thailand). ASEAN did not have any document upon which to build a foundational understanding of human rights until the ASEAN Charter (2009), forty-two years after ASEAN's formation.

The Recent Past

ASEAN's approach towards human rights issues differs from the EU, and this may create certain misunderstandings or misgivings. In earlier years, there was not a sufficient understanding on both sides how each other stood. Especially problematic was the 1990s, when the EU and ASEAN first began to discuss human rights issues. The EU wanted to mainstream human rights — the principle of conditionality applied not just to nations seeking to accede to the EU, but also generally with all other nations it had dealings with. Respect for human rights and democratic values therefore (quite understandably from the EU's point of view) had to be a core principle underpinning its relations with ASEAN. The EU also wanted to link economic cooperation with progress on the human rights front. Another source of tension came from the positions taken by some EU nations (and NGOs based within the EU) that pressure (including economic pressure) should be brought to bear on ASEAN to do more on human rights or specific issues on Myanmar or other issues such as death penalty.

The model of putting pressure on ASEAN in this way did not work and was counterproductive. As one commentator, Maria Gabriela-Manea, observed in 2008,

Human rights policy interaction has been carried out mainly in a rhetorical mode of interaction that has been, for the most part, confrontational, but has more recently changed into

strategic accommodation. Furthermore, interregional dialogue has established two informal arenas in which communicative modes of interaction have become prevalent. This has [two] implications for the collective identity of ASEAN. On the one hand, it has given ASEAN the incentive to engage in setting boundaries and defining itself as something contrary or different from the European Union. This has led to its critical and inflexible stance on human rights issues when communicating with the European Union, but it has also caused a hegemonic discourse on 'Asian values' to grow within ASEAN, a discourse that dominated the internal policy landscape up until the Asian financial crisis.

Only after ASEAN had achieved degree of stability and expanded its membership (in the form of accepting Cambodia, Myanmar, Laos and Vietnam into the grouping) did AMS begin, in their fourth decade, to discuss human rights. In November 2007 saw the signing of the ASEAN Charter, the preamble of which states that ASEAN members are 'adhering to the principles of democracy, the rule of law and good governance, respect for and protection of human rights and fundamental freedoms.'

Article 14 of the Charter stipulates that 'ASEAN shall establish an ASEAN human rights body', which in 2009 would come into being in the form of AICHR. AICHR in turn began drafting an ASEAN Human Rights Declaration (AHRD) in 2011. This was adopted in 2012. This in itself was something of an achievement. Catherine Ashton, High Representative of the EU for Foreign Affairs and Security Policy, called the Declaration "an important step towards strengthening the protection of human rights in Asia."

The AHRD affirms that the UN Declaration of Human Rights is universal. It should not be considered surprising, however, that the AHRD makes reference to subjecting human rights standards to national laws, local cultures, and public morality. Nor is the AHRD legally binding on AMS. The AHRD is concerned more with the notion of promotion of Human Rights, rather than "protection" in the sense that it is commonly understood in the West. This has occasioned some disappointment in some quarters in the West and in the EU.

Some observers in the EU rue the fact that ASEAN has elected to proceed in its own way (and at its own pace) on human rights issues. It might be more profitable, however, to turn future discussions to concrete issues where cooperation and comparing notes is badly needed. Certain things have happened around the world which have impacted both in the EU (and in the West generally) and ASEAN. Some EU nations have had to think hard about whether their policies (and here I include human rights considerations) are adequate for dealing with these issues that have arisen.

(Dis)information

One area that ASEAN and the EU can find common ground in is the fight against disinformation and fake news. The right to high quality information should be considered an essential human right, and this should be an issue that brings ASEAN and EU together.

The EU recognises (clearly evidenced through its official publications) that disinformation and propaganda have a direct impact on human rights, the rule of law, and democracy. At the same time, Article 10 of the European Convention on Human Rights states that everyone has the right to freedom of expression, and that this right shall include freedom to hold opinions and to receive and impart information and ideas without interference. But Article 10 goes on to note that:

"The exercise of these freedoms, since it carries with it duties and responsibilities, may be subject to such formalities, conditions, restrictions or penalties as are prescribed by law and are necessary in a democratic society, in the interests of national security, territorial integrity or public safety, for the prevention of disorder or crime, for the protection of health or morals, for the protection of the reputation or rights of others, for preventing the disclosure of information received in confidence, or for maintaining the authority and impartiality of the judiciary."

I would suggest that this approach is in fact not that much different from the positions taken by various AMS. Some AMS have enacted their own legislation in the recent past with the aim, either wholly or in part, of fighting fake news and disinformation. These include Vietnam, Thailand, and Singapore. While the laws these AMS have enacted are very different, what they have in common is the attempt to limit poor quality information and mitigate its impact on society.

These laws are necessary — and here again there is common ground across ASEAN and the EU — because suasion with the tech companies and softer measures have not worked. The EU for example launched in late 2018 the EU Code of Practice (COP) on Disinformation for a trial period of twelve months. The COP relied in the first instance on trust and self-regulations between the key players (government, tech companies), with the emphasis on voluntary collaboration on the part of the tech companies running social networks. As laudable as initiatives like the COP have been, they have not proved sufficient to stem the flow of fake news and disinformation, which threatens to undermine the resilience of societies.

We have much to learn from each other when it comes to ensuring access to information while at the same time balancing this freedom with the freedom of societies to be free from forces that might seek to undermine them through fake news and disinformation.

Intolerance

It is intolerance that may well prove to be the threat of our times across both east and west.

The foment created by social media has not resulted in one single happy online global village. It is undeniable that while the contestation of ideas online can be a force for good, it has also meant that people have become more intolerant, locked into their own filter bubbles and echo chambers. Intolerant ideologies and exclusivist thought is on the rise in Europe just as it is in Asia (and AMS are not immune from this).

There are various European initiatives to address this issue. These include the Council of Europe's "no-hate-speech" campaign to raise the awareness of the danger of using hate speech and encourage politicians to avoid inflammatory rhetoric. The EU itself has a High-Level Group on Combatting Racism, Xenophobia and other forms of Intolerance.

At the EU-AICHR Policy Dialogue on Human Rights in Brussels in November 2019, there was useful preliminary discussion of this — how the young generation who carry the torch will need to understand tolerance, common space, and pluralism. It is the right of citizens of AMS to have enjoy these conditions, just as it is in EU nations. But these things that we have for so long taken for granted as ingrained into our societies are increasingly under threat. These are issues that the EU and ASEAN should actively consult and compare notes on, with the aim of building a muscular defence of what we hold dear — tolerance and moderation.

Going Forward

Preserving a common space is going to be critical even as nations seek to uphold the values of tolerance and moderation.

To discuss these issues frankly and in a constructive manner, common space is also needed between the EU and ASEAN.

On paper, the EU and ASEAN already have mechanisms to exchange views these issues specifically and human rights issues in general. The ASEAN Intergovernmental Commission on Human Rights (AICHR) conducts regular meetings with the EU. AICHR also interacts with CSOs from the region and further afield — AICHR might not always agree with their points of view, but the need to have continued dialogue and engagement is recognised. Finally, AICHR has a key a role in the Universal Periodic Review (UPR) process conducted by the UN Human Rights Council (which itself has mechanisms for CSOs and other interested parties to give input).

These interactions when they take place should be in an atmosphere of mutual respect — it is only in this type of setting that ideas and best practices on the issues above can be exchanged. Could continued interaction in a constructive atmosphere help to shape thinking in some of these issues in ASEAN and within AMS? Possibly, just as the EU may over time better understand that what some AMS states are doing in various issues (such as those highlighted above) is actually to forge a path that works for them. These pathways are not set in stone. When it comes to rights, state approaches evolve over time even as their own societies mature.

In these interactions, it is inevitable that there will be occasional frustrations. But both sides should understand — and the evidence of recent years would suggest that this understanding is present — that it is far better to keep the lines of communication open.

7

Convergence and Divergence
ASEAN's and the EU's Responses to the Rohingya Crisis

Noeleen Heyzer and Lilianne Fan

This essay explores the respective responses of ASEAN and the European Union to the Rohingya crisis. While the crisis has not been ignored by either regional body, the responses by ASEAN and the EU have to a large extent been determined by a) the particular frameworks, tools and mechanisms that exist within each regional organisation, and b) the political will, or lack thereof, of member states to address the crisis.

A People Without a State

The Rohingya, a Muslim minority in Myanmar's Rakhine State, have long been one of the world's most vulnerable communities, affected by multiple forms of denial of basic human rights, dispossession, displacement and violence over many decades. Effectively rendered stateless by Myanmar's 1982 Citizenship Law, which grants citizenship only to 135 officially recognised ethnic groups, the Rohingya currently constitute the largest stateless population in the world. It is this condition of statelessness that lies at the root of Myanmar's denial of basic human rights and protections towards the Rohingya population.

Without the ability to obtain nationality and civic documentation, Rohingya cannot access basic services such as education and healthcare, are denied the right to family life, and face severe restrictions on freedom of movement and livelihoods. The lack of recognition as citizens has also subjected Rohingya to multiple and extreme forms of violence, from arbitrary arrest and forced labour to mass atrocities, the latter of which have led to allegations of genocide at the International Court of Justice and crimes against humanity at the International Criminal Court. These conditions have led to a protracted regional refugee crisis, with over 2 million Rohingya seeking protection across the region, in countries such as Bangladesh, Malaysia, Indonesia, Thailand, India and Pakistan.

The situation of the Rohingya must be understood in the wider context of both Myanmar and Rakhine State. Over the past decade, even as Myanmar was undergoing its historic democratic transition from military to civilian rule and opening up to the regional and international community after years of isolation. Rakhine State has experienced a steady rise of conflict, violence and socio-economic insecurity, and is today not only one of the country's poorest states but also one of the most conflict affected, with the armed conflict between the Arakan Army and the Myanmar Military intensifying since 2019. The escalating conflict in Rakhine has both immediate and long-term implications for the situation of the Rohingya who remain in Rakhine State as well as the prospects for safe, voluntary and dignified return for Rohingya who fled Rakhine to seek refuge across the border in Bangladesh and across the region.

Between Principles and Political Will

The Association of Southeast Asian Nations (ASEAN) and the European Union (EU) have both responded to the Rohingya crisis. However, while there are some points of convergence in some areas of these responses, for the most part these approaches have been framed in fundamentally different ways, and have been determined, facilitated and limited by the particular principles, mandates and politics of each regional organisation.

For ASEAN, the Rohingya crisis can only be officially addressed through the regional platform on terms agreed to by Myanmar, which is a member state of ASEAN. ASEAN's approach has been one of engaging constructively with Myanmar as a member of the 'ASEAN family' in the 'ASEAN Way', trying to influence change from within, rather than confronting, condemning or holding Myanmar to account publicly on the human rights situation in Rakhine. ASEAN's lack of public criticism on the human rights situation in Rakhine State, however, obscures the reality that a number of ASEAN member states, particularly Malaysia and Indonesia, have expressed concerns over the human rights situation for many years and have attempted to raise the issue at ASEAN Foreign Ministers' Meetings. One member state in particular, namely Malaysia, has in recent years played a leading role in defending Rohingya rights and condemning violence against the community at the highest global levels, including the United Nations General Assembly and the Organisation for Islamic Cooperation (OIC). However, because of the principles of consensus and non-interference, ASEAN member states have only succeeded in using the ASEAN platform, as opposed to other platforms, to address humanitarian and development dimensions of the crisis.

ASEAN's own human rights mechanism, the ASEAN Intergovernmental Commission for Human Rights (AICHR) has not raised the issue formally, although it has been proposed by several representatives, due to a lack of approval from Myanmar. Nonetheless, ASEAN leaders were aware of the importance of ASEAN response to the crisis. In 2018 ASEAN managed to convince Myanmar to allow the ASEAN Coordinating Centre for Humanitarian Assistance (AHA Centre) to conduct a preliminary needs assessment in Rakhine State to facilitate repatriation of Rohingya refugees from Bangladesh and to seek opportunities for ASEAN cooperation to improve conditions in Rakhine State. ASEAN Chairman's Statements in 2018 and 2019 also stated the need for durable solutions to the crisis and for accountability, using much stronger language than had previously been seen in official ASEAN statements. The engagement by ASEAN in the crisis also led to two facilitated dialogue sessions between Government of Myanmar representatives and Rohingya refugees in Cox's Bazar. In late 2019, the Secretary General of ASEAN established the Ad-Hoc Support Team of the ASEAN Secretary-General (AHAST) to implement the findings of the Preliminary Needs Assessment, another indication that ASEAN increasingly views the Rohingya crisis and its implications for the region with seriousness.

While ASEAN continues to address the Rohingya crisis primarily as a humanitarian crisis, in contrast, the European Union frames the Rohingya crisis as first and foremost a human rights crisis, one that has led to serious humanitarian consequences. By December 2019, the EU has provided over EUR 140 million in humanitarian and recovery assistance to the Rohingya refugee crisis in Bangladesh alone. The EU also provides support to humanitarian and development efforts in Rakhine State, Myanmar, and regularly mobilises its diplomatic offices to advocate the Myanmar Government to address the crisis. The EU sees this as a regional refugee crisis and hence the need to enhance protection for Rohingya refugees across the region.

The differences in approach are largely determined by the very different historical contexts, mandates and frameworks that underpin ASEAN and the EU as regional bodies. Modern Europe was founded on the very principles of human rights in the aftermath of the horrors of World War II. By the time the European Union was formally established in 1993, there was already the existence of robust, layered and independent human rights institutions, treaties and mechanisms in Europe. These include the Council of Europe, established in 1949, the

European Court of Human Rights and the European Committee of Social Rights, as well as the Council of Europe Commissioner for Human Rights, underpinned by the European Convention on Human Rights and other binding legal frameworks.

The EU also differs from ASEAN in that it is a supranational regional entity where Member States have pooled their sovereignty into common institutions, laws and policies. ASEAN is a regional intergovernmental organisation in which cooperation is based on consensus and protection of sovereignty, rather than integration and subjugation to legally binding regional norms and standards.

However, notwithstanding its strong human rights foundation, significant contributions as a humanitarian, peace and development donor, and high-level diplomatic efforts, the EU has, arguably, had little real political influence on the Government of Myanmar on the Rohingya crisis and improving conditions in Rakhine State. As for ASEAN, while it lacks robust and legally binding human rights frameworks and institutions to address the crisis, it has demonstrated that with the right political will it can mobilise regional humanitarian and security diplomacy in a way that Myanmar is willing to engage. The question remains, however, what impact either of these approaches will have in the long-term on the situation of the Rohingya and whether progress will truly be made either in resolving the root causes of the crisis in Myanmar or effectively advancing the protection of Rohingya refugees in the wider region.

Part Three

Diverse and Evolving Bilateral Ties

8

Brunei Darussalam-European Union Relations
Moving Beyond Diplomatic Niceties

Osman Patra

An Overview of Brunei-EU Relations

Brunei Darussalam (Brunei) and the European Union (EU) established diplomatic relations in 1989 when the latter was still the European Economic Community (EEC). The development of bilateral relations was enhanced by concurrent accreditation of a Bruneian Ambassador to Belgium in Brussels as Ambassador to the EU. In recent years, the EU reciprocated with the accreditation of the EU Ambassador in Jakarta to Brunei. The day-to-day interests of the EU in Brunei are represented by France and Germany, the two EU member states which have missions based in the capital of Brunei, on six-monthly rotational basis. Since the resumption of its independence in 1984, Brunei has established diplomatic ties with most of the member states of the EU.

Over the years, relationship remains friendly and cordial. There has not been any serious problem detected either with any individual EU member states or with the EU itself. The Head of State and Government of Brunei Darussalam also contributed to the strengthening of bilateral relations through occasional visits to the EU institutions in Brussels. Furthermore, frequent exchanges of working visits have been taking place between officials of Brunei and EU. Merchandise trade between the two entities amounts to €740 million in 2018 and consists of machineries, motor vehicles and chemicals. The trade is in the EU's favour.[1] The volume is still much smaller compared to most of the ASEAN countries.[2]

The other significant area of cooperation is in education where a few thousands of the country's young people obtained their higher and professional education, particularly from the United Kingdom. The on-going policy of the Bruneian Government to diversify its economy especially in non-oil and gas industries, tourism, financial and banking services and efforts to improve the nation's infrastructure offers vast potential for stronger economic ties between the two.

In recent years, Brunei and the EU had also launched discussions on a Partnership Cooperation Agreement (PCA) to strengthen cooperation. The conclusion of the PCA would be an important step towards a bilateral free trade arrangement between them. The last round of PCA discussions took place in 2014. The prospect for the discussions to resume appears more difficult now. Complicated issues, such as the possibility of issuing joint statement on human rights; and EU's concern on the implementation of the Sharia Law Penal Code,[3] represent some of the obstacles in moving forward.

The absence of any bilateral cooperation agreement, though not unique to Brunei only, is compensated by Brunei's participation in cooperative activities under the aegis of the ASEAN-EU dialogue and the Asia-Europe Meeting (ASEM) platform. The EU's interest in ASEAN has been strengthened with the appointment of a separate EU ambassador accredited to ASEAN. The enhanced EU-ASEAN cooperation is beneficial also to the development of bilateral ties between Brunei and the EU.

---

[1] For details of bilateral trade figures, European Commission, Directorate-General for Trade, 2018.

[2] ASEAN Key Figures 2019, ASEAN Secretariat, (https//:www.asean.org), pp. 29–38.

[3] Eileen Ng in *The Straits Times*, "Brunei Says Syariah Law Not Meant To Discriminate", 13 April 2019.

From the foregoing discussion, it is instructive that the depth of relationship between the two entities while distantly friendly still leaves a lot of room for improvement and visibility. The pace of cooperation tends to move in a piecemeal manner, unstructured and frequently on a 'tag along' basis when the EU implements certain activities or even a simple working visit by senior officials to a few ASEAN member countries. In view of the exit of the United Kingdom from the EU earlier this year, whom Brunei has long history of ties and wide range of cooperation, the extent of the country's dealings with the EU would likely be affected.[4]

Brunei-EU Relations within the ASEAN-EU Framework: Priorities and Interests

In contrast to the bilateral ties, Brunei's engagement with the EU at the inter-regional level seems to be more robust. Brunei joined ASEAN in January 1984, and automatically became a member of the ASEAN-EC Dialogue process. Brunei has consistently been an active participant of the Dialogue meetings and cooperative activities. Despite this, the country had only acceded to the ASEAN-EEC Cooperation Agreement of 1980 through an instrument of extension, signed in November 1994, as the 6th member of ASEAN. Since joining the dialogue framework, it has not been able to fully benefit from the many EC projects available due to the GDP income threshold condition rendering it ineligible for the EC provision of development assistance. Nevertheless, they continue to find ways to work together through a co-funding arrangement.

For instance, in 1994, Brunei and EC together implemented a joint project with each contributing ECUs 2,268,926

---

[4] Richard Lindsay, "Brexit will not impact UK relations with Brunei", Borneo Bulletin, 1st February 2020.

ECUs 1,973,400, respectively to set up the ASEAN-EC Management Centre aimed at promoting a centre of excellence on management and policy dialogue.[5] With the in-kind co-funding arrangement, a new building and sufficient staffing were provided for the Centre and beneficial activities were held for a number of years. The project had not proceeded to the level that both sides could be satisfied with. Nevertheless it provided numerous useful lessons and experience especially for Brunei on how to work pragmatically together.

In examining the reasons for the current state of Brunei-EU relations, it is necessary to understand whether the differing background, interests, values and strategic position and priority of each entity, hinder the development of more vigorous ties. In the case of Brunei, the quintessential characteristics of the EU could be a more formidable peculiarity to surmount. Admittedly even at the wider regional stage there always exist frequent acrimonious interactions and complexities emanating from the fact that the EU is supranational and rules-based while ASEAN is inter-governmental in structure with emphasis on principle of non-interference and a consensus-based decision making.

In spite of these differences, inter-regional cooperation have deepened. This is evidenced by the intensity of dialogue across all areas of mutual interest; regular new political and strategic pronouncements, commitment by leaders and ministers; and the steady support structures of the ASEAN-EU process. Moreover, this also reaffirms the EU's preference in working with the region through the inter-regional framework.[6] Unfortunately, this also meant EU placed less attention on the bilateral relationship with

---

[5] "Financing Memorandum Between the EC and The Government of Brunei Darussalam, Cebu, the Philippines, 1994, ASEAN Secretariat, External Relations.

[6] Jorn Dosh and Naila Maier-Knap, "EU-ASEAN Relations: Taking Stock of a Comprehensive Inter-Regional Relationship Between Natural Partners", in PANORAMA 01/2017, Konrad Adenauer Stiftung, pp.125–138.

Brunei. A reset approach is required to promote a more substantive bilateral relationship which at the same time reinforces the effectiveness of inter-regional processes.

Since the resumption of its full independence in 1984, the initial phase of Brunei's foreign policy objectives among others was to gain political recognition by as many countries as possible. Another priority is to make rapid progress in its overall development particularly through its program of economic diversification. The paramount objective inevitably lies in the nation's preoccupation with its security, viability and survival as a political and an independent entity.[7]

After gaining the recognition by the 5 Permanent Members of the United Nations Security Council following its acceptance as a new member of the United Nations, Brunei sought to establish diplomatic relations with all P5 members, notably the United Kingdom and France which possess global strategic outreach and military capabilities. Ties with China and Russia were only set up in 1991.

Brunei's accession into ASEAN in early 1984 and its induction into the ASEAN-EC dialogue engendered not only the EU's direct support and recognition that bolster greater legitimacy to its status as an independent country, but also provides opportunities for greater cooperation This, together with the setting up of ties with other EU member states potentially offer significant political, economic and strategic opportunities for Brunei either bilaterally or multilaterally.

In the meantime, the EU has further established its presence as a positive force in the overall development of the region. Although for the EU the economic and trade activities will remain an overriding interest in its external ties, significant changes in the past decades also saw the EU increasingly pursuing its position as a global security player. This is further assisted when the

---

[7] Chin and Suryadinata, "Michael Leifer: Selected Work on Southeast Asia", pp. 657–671, ISEAS, 2005.

so-called 'donor-recipient' relationship has overtime evolved into an equal partnership between the two organisations as ASEAN charted its path towards becoming a full-fledge Community and a prominent economic and political grouping in Asia.

Brunei has played an important role in bringing the status of ASEAN-EU Dialogue into what it is today; spurring the adjustment in emphasis from development cooperation to closer collaboration in trade and economic areas and supporting the consensus for greater EU's role in political and security affairs of the region through ASEAN's led processes. This also includes the co-sponsoring of the launch of the Asia-Europe Meeting (ASEM) in 1996.

Beyond Diplomatic Niceties

In view of the strategic and more pragmatically nuance adjustment of EU's approach towards ASEAN in recent years, stronger commensurate actions need to be introduced to close the potential gaps in the inter-regional ASEAN-EU process. The EU has acknowledged the critical importance of good relations with individual ASEAN member states for further progress in the inter-regional Dialogue.[8] However, it still has no further distinctive proposals aimed at ensuring that 'no individual ASEAN member country is left behind'. Commitment to the less developed ASEAN member states would certainly continue. Under the ARISE Plus Program, projects are allocated to most of ASEAN countries except for Brunei and Singapore. Brunei's involvement in these projects has been quite circumscribed and has contributed to the implementation of ASEAN-EU initiatives through participation on voluntary basis.[9]

In making the current state of Brunei-EU ties more purposeful, the two sides must establish a strategic theme which defines

---

[8] Yeo Lay Hwee, "ASEAN's Cooperation with the European Union — ASEM and Beyond", *ASEAN at 50: A Look at Its External Relations*, Konrad Adenauer Stiftung, pp. 81–93.

[9] Blue Book 2019, EU-ASEAN Cooperation.

their long-term relations. To achieve this, engaging the country in a consistent dialogue is pre-requisite to really understand the kind of preoccupation the Bruneians are seized with. For Brunei, acquisition of knowledge, expertise and best practices from the EU will upgrade Brunei's capacities to deliver on its own socioeconomic priorities. The EU is well-known for policy dialogues and advisory activities in capacities and competencies building; trade and investments; technology; and political and security cooperation. Looking ahead, the two sides can establish beneficial exchanges through a better structured mode of dialogue by setting up a bilateral 'framework' at the Ministerial or Secretary General level to enhance and coordinate multifaceted cooperative activities. Brunei's vision 2035 has been introduced in response to the slowing of economic growth in recent decades as well as a comprehensive attempt at addressing future socio-economic aspirations of the country. This vision should be a catalyst to turn the corner in its relations with the EU.

Brunei has special interest in promoting linkages between the young people in Southeast Asia and Europe especially through educational exchanges and environmental protection activities. The country has regularly expressed strong desire to invite students or researchers from the EU to undertake study in Brunei in the general academic areas or undertake research pertaining to the rain forest, especially through the 'Heart of Borneo' initiative. Perhaps the EU's new 'differentiated' approach could make collaboration in these areas strongly possible.[10]

An enduring and multifaceted relationship shared by both sides has to be underpinned by a deep understanding of each other's unique cultural values and position on matters of common interest through promoting appropriate adaptation rather than accentuating inherent differences. It is crucial that the EU appreciates the unique position of Brunei as a truly moderate

---

[10] op cit.

yet modern Islamic country that it could count on as partner in addressing many of the regional and international issues of concern, and not as harshly caricatured by certain mainstream media or interest groups.[11] The episode which occurred last year whereby the EU Parliament approved a resolution condemning the passage of the Sharia Law Penal Code resulted in difficulties affecting business, education and ability of Brunei to deal with many European institutions.[12] The EU countries open condemnation of the Brunei's human rights record in the Geneva Universal Periodic Review in 2019 was another case in point. More dialogue would have helped to put the matter in a more appropriate perspective. At the Periodic Review, an overwhelming number of countries had praised Brunei's human rights records and the improvement it had made in many aspects.[13]

The discussions above capture some salient features of the Brunei-EU bilateral relationship underscoring possible explanations for its lackluster. At the same time the seemingly impressive participation at the ASEAN-EU process, while very useful diplomatically, is also fraught with inherent difficulties. Furthermore, this may gloss over the limited work at the country level. In this regard, careful consideration should be given to Brunei's unique situation especially the multifaceted challenges which a small state normally faces in interacting with bigger countries or organisations. The casualness in taking this into account, probably explains the limited appreciation of the bigger partner's long-term consideration in pursuing stronger engagement with the country. Brunei's valuable relations with the EU bilaterally and through ASEAN-EU has served its interest

---

[11] Din Al-Burnawi, "Check Facts, Circumstances Before Pushing Agenda", Borneo Bulletin, 25th May 2019.
[12] European Parliament Resolution of 18/04/2019 on Brunei, (2019/2692(RSP)).
[13] UN Watch, "Brunei Praised in the Human Rights Review Despite Implementation of the Sharia Penal Code", 10th May 2019.

well since the resumption of its independence, and for the future this will be even more critical. In moving forward, there needs to be mutual desire to intensify relations beyond mere diplomatic necessity.

9

Cambodia-EU Relations
Beyond Everything-but-Arms

Chheang Vannarith

Introduction

The European Union (EU) has played quite an important role in assisting the ASEAN member states, especially Cambodia, Laos, Vietnam and Myanmar, to develop their economies and integrate into the regional economy. Cambodia regards the EU as one of its key development and trading partners. The total trade in goods between the two partners equalled €6.2 billion (USD 7 billion) in 2018, accounting for 17.3% of Cambodia's total trade. However, the differences over human rights and democracy, especially in recent years, have put certain stress and constraints on the bilateral relations.

On 12 February 2020, the EU decided to partially remove Cambodia from the Everything-But-Arms (EBA) preferential trade scheme - due to concerns over Cambodia's violation of political rights and restrictive actions on civil society and trade union. The Cambodian government responded by calling the EU's decision "double standards". This essay sheds light on the dynamics of Cambodia-EU relations from the perspective of a small state focused on development and regime survival.

Overview of Cambodia-EU Relations

Cambodia-EU relations was established in 1994. The bilateral cooperation agreement was signed in 1997 and came into effect in 1999. The Cambodia-EU Joint Committee (JC) was established to ensure smooth and effective implementation of the Agreement. The Joint Committee holds its meeting every two years and each side takes turn to host the session on a rotational basis. There had been ten meetings so far. The 11th meeting to be hosted by Cambodia on 16-18 March 2020 was cancelled by the EU side due to the concern over Covid-19 outbreak.

Since 1992, the EU has supported Cambodia on hundreds of projects focused on bringing up the level of socio-economic development in areas from education to health. And in 2007, the EU initiated the framework agreement on Multi-Annual Indicative Program (MIP) to support a wider area of cooperation with Cambodia. The agreement on MIP has been implemented in three phases. From 2007 to 2010, the EU provided grants of up to €77 million (USD 87.5 million) focusing on governance, trade, education, and human rights. From 2011 to 2013, the EU's €83 million grants continued its focus on education, governance, and trade, but also adding new focus on agriculture and public financial management. As a sign of EU's continued engagement on Cambodia's development, from 2014 to 2020, the EU committed a substantive grant of €410 million (USD466 million) focusing on agriculture, natural resources management (fisheries and forestry), education and skills development, and governance and public administration.

In 2019, the EU and the Council for the Development of Cambodia (CDC) held a consultative meeting to align the EU's development cooperation strategy with the development strategies of the Cambodian government. The joint strategy developed after the consultative meeting identified five priority areas, namely governance; equitable and sustainable economic growth; physical infrastructure development; skills development, employment generation and human resource development.

Beyond pragmatic developmental cooperation, the EU also provided grants to support political transition and electoral process in Cambodia. About €30 million (USD34 million) was given to support the Extraordinary Chambers in the Court of Cambodia (ECCC) for the Khmer Rouge trial. Support for the election process in Cambodia amounted to €18 million (USD20.46 million) from 1998 to 2016. However, in 2017, the EU suspended its electoral support to Cambodia after the main opposition party, the Cambodia National Rescue Party (CNRP), was dissolved by the Supreme Court.

Bilateral trade between Cambodia and the EU increased significantly thanks to the Everything But Arms (EBA) preferential tariff scheme that the EU granted to Cambodia in 2001. Cambodia's garment industry benefitted tremendously from the EBA scheme. 40% of what is produced by the garment industry in Cambodia goes to the EU. This is followed by the United States (30%).[1] The garment industry is an important part of the Cambodian economy employing about 800,000 workers, nearly 80 percent of whom are women.[2] Another important Cambodian export to the EU is bicycle. In 2018, 1.52 million bicycles were exported from Cambodia to the EU.

In the agricultural sector, Cambodia exports around 300,000 metric tons of rice to the EU market. However, in a protectionist move to safeguard the market share of EU producers, the European Commission launched safeguard measure on the import of Indica rice from Cambodia into the EU market. In January 2019, the EU went ahead with the safeguard measures

---

[1] ASEAN Briefing, https://www.aseanbriefing.com/news/cambodias-garment-manufacturing-industry/

[2] International Labour Organization (ILO), Living conditions of garment and footwear sector workers in Cambodia. Cambodia Garment and Footwear Sector Bulletin, Issue 8, December 2018.

on rice from Cambodia and Myanmar and set a duty of €175 (USD198.88) per tonne in the first year, €150 (USD170.47) in the second year, and €125 (USD142.06) in the third year. The tariffs were imposed as increased imports of Indica rice from these two countries had affected the market share of the EU producers — it dropped from 61 percent to 29 percent.[3] The safeguard measure has affected the livelihoods of half a million Cambodian farmers.[4]

This brief overview of Cambodia's relations with the EU reflects the dilemma that small states face in its external relations. On the one hand, the EU has been a steadfast developmental partner of Cambodia; on the other hand, small states such as Cambodia are also particularly sensitive to any affront to its sovereignty and interference in its domestic affairs. This brings us to examine more closely in the next section how Cambodia's exercise of small state diplomacy may mean for the future of Cambodia's relations with the EU.

Cambodia and Small State Diplomacy

Small states are susceptible to external changes and foreign intervention. Due to limited resources and capability, small states have to rely on external sources for growth. Hence international integration is usually one of the key foreign policy objectives and interests of small states. Cambodia adopted a neutral and independent foreign policy after it gained independence from France in 1953. However, it was forced to take sides and became the victim of great power politics during the Cold War era.

At the end of the Cold War and with the establishment of the Second Kingdom in 1993, Cambodia began its pursuit of

---

[3] "Cambodia takes EU to court over rice import tariffs", Reuters 11 April 2019. https://www.reuters.com/article/us-eu-cambodia-rice/cambodia-takes-eu-to-court-over-rice-import-tariffs-idUSKCN1RN17S

[4] "Cambodia says EU's rice tariffs affect half mln farmer-families", Xinhua News, 22 August 2019. http://www.xinhuanet.com/english/2019-08/22/c_138329495.htm

a pragmatic foreign policy. It implemented an omni-directional foreign policy strategy underpin by economic pragmatism and soft balancing.[5] Cambodia actively pursues strategic diversification and tries to maintain good and stable relationships with all major powers. As a small power, it is also in Cambodia's interest to support multilateralism and uphold a rules-based international order. Prime Minister Hun Sen, at the 25th International Conference on the Future of Asia in Tokyo in 2019, said that, Cambodia is against protectionism and unilateralism as these political ideologies hinder global progress and disrupt the open multilateral system. Promoting and advancing open and inclusive multilateralism serve the interests of all.[6] Addressing the World Summit 2020 in Seoul, Prime Minister Hun Sen again stressed the importance of strengthening international cooperation and embracing an open and inclusive multilateral trading system, globalisation and international connectivity.[7]

As stipulated in the 1993 Constitution, Cambodia adheres to six foreign policy principles. First, Cambodia adopts a policy of permanent neutrality and non-alignment. Second, it follows a policy of peaceful co-existence with its neighbours and with all other countries throughout the world. Third, it shall not invade any country, nor interfere in any other country's internal affairs—directly or indirectly—and shall solve any problem peacefully with due respect for mutual interest. Fourth, it shall not join any military alliance or military pact which is incompatible with its policy of neutrality. Fifth, it shall not permit any foreign military base on its territory and shall not have its own military

---

[5] Leng, Thearith (2016) Small state diplomacy: Cambodia's foreign policy towards Vietnam. *The Pacific Review* DOI: 10.1080/09512748.2016.1239128.

[6] Chheang Vannarith (2019) Cambodia's worldview 2019. Khmer Times, 5 June 2019, https://www.khmertimeskh.com/50610950/cambodias-worldview-2019/

[7] Khmer Times. "Cambodia's four-point proposals to promote world peace". 4 February 2020. https://www.khmertimeskh.com/50687161/cambodias-four-point-proposals-to-promote-world-peace

base abroad, except within the framework of a United Nations request. Sixth, it reserves the right to receive foreign assistance in military equipment, armaments, ammunition, training of its armed forces, and other assistance for self-defence, to maintain public order and security within its territory.

Cambodia's worldview is in favour of multilateralism with the UN-centred international system staying at the core especially with regard to the respect of national sovereignty and non-interference.[8] Cambodia's foreign policy strategy has been chiefly shaped and driven by "economic pragmatism," meaning the alignment of foreign policy with economic development interests. The Cambodian government's two main approaches to regional economic integration are (1) leveraging the international environment for national development and (2) diversifying strategic partnerships based on the calculation of economic interests. International economic cooperation and regional integration are key principles of Cambodia's foreign policy, which emphasizes shared development and win-win cooperation.[9]

For Cambodia, economic security is considered as national security. Foreign policy is regarded as a tool to serve Cambodia's national economic development and safeguard its economic interest. In early 2020, Cambodia has engaged in proactive economic diplomacy to further attract foreign direct investment, promote export, and develop its tourism industry. Therefore, Cambodia's relations with the EU is driven very much by economic imperatives. The EU's removal of Cambodia from its EBA preferential tariff scheme is thus a big blow to Cambodia.

---

[8] Chheang Vannarith (2019) "Cambodia's worldview 2019", Khmer Times, 5 June 2019, https://www.khmertimeskh.com/50610950/cambodias-worldview-2019/

[9] Chheang, Vannarith (2018) "Economic pragmatism and regional economic integration: The case of Cambodia", Asia Pacific Bulletin No. 429, East-West Center. https://www.eastwestcenter.org/publications/economic-pragmatism-and-regional-economic-integration-the-case-cambodia

EBA and Future of Cambodia-EU Relations

In 2001, the EU adopted a resolution on Everything-but-Arms (EBA) scheme to allow duty-free and quota-free access to the EU for all exports from the least developed countries except arms. As a least developed country, Cambodia was included in the EBA scheme with human rights and labour conditionality. Since then Cambodia has enjoyed tariff and quota free exports to the EU market. The EBA tariff preferences have had a remarkable impact on economic growth and jobs in Cambodia. Cambodia is the second largest beneficiary of EBA preferences after Bangladesh. The EU has become Cambodia's largest trading partner, accounting for 45% of its total exports in 2018. Exports from Cambodia to the EU reached €5.4 billion (USD6.14 billion) in 2018- 95.7% of these exports entered the EU market under EBA scheme, equalling to €5.2 billion (USD5.91 billion) out of the total €5.4 billion (USD6.14 billion).[10]

After the arrest of the opposition leader, Kem Sokha on 2 September 2017, and the dissolution of the main opposition party, Cambodia National Rescue Party (CNRP), on 16 November 2017, the EU warned that Cambodia risked being taken out of the EBA scheme for its backsliding on democracy and human rights. Since then, both parties have engaged in intensive dialogue to resolve the issue.

In February 2018, the EU Foreign Affairs Council issued a statement expressing concerns over political development in Cambodia, especially with regards to the respect of human rights and fundamental freedoms. In June 2018, Cambodia sent a goodwill mission to Brussels to explain the real situation in Cambodia. In July 2018, the EU sent a Monitoring Mission to Cambodia to further assess the situation in Cambodia. In August

---

[10] European Commission, Trade/Human Rights: withdrawal of Cambodia's preferential access to the EU market—Factsheet. https://trade.ec.europa.eu/doclib/docs/2020/february/tradoc_158631.pdf

2018, Cambodia submitted its full responses to the EU's questionnaires on EBA Enhanced Engagement. In October 2018, Cambodia's PM Hun Sen met with the EU High Representative for Foreign Affairs and Security Policy Federica Mogherini on the side-line of the 12th ASEM Summit to try and reach an understanding on the political development in Cambodia. In December 2018, Cambodia dispatched another goodwill mission to Brussels to continue its dialogue. At the same time, the Ministry of Foreign Affairs and International Cooperation issued a statement explaining concrete measures to improve human rights and democracy in Cambodia. In January 2019, Foreign Minister Prak Sokhonn met with the EU Commissioner for Trade, Ms Cecilla Malmstrom.

Despite the flurry of meetings, the EU was not convinced by the steps taken and the explanations from Cambodia and decided in February 2019 to launch a formal procedure to temporarily suspend EBA. In March 2019, Cambodia received the EU delegation to continue dialogue on EBA. In August 2019, Foreign Minister Prak Sokhonn met with Mogherini on the side-line of ASEAN Ministerial Meeting in Bangkok. In the same month, Cambodia provided consolidated responses to the EC's Note to the File regarding "EBA Enhanced Engagement-Cambodia". In October 2019, Cambodia dispatched its third mission to seven EU member countries (France, Germany, Spain, Italy, Belgium, Poland and Portugal) to explain the progress made by Cambodia with regards to civil society space, labour rights, and land issues in Cambodia. In November 2019, Cambodia received the EU Commission Report of Findings and Conclusions. In December 2019, Cambodia provided response to the report.

PM Hun Sen has warned several times that should the EU decide to remove Cambodia from the EBA scheme, the EU would have no room to talk about human rights and democracy in Cambodia.[11] China has expressed support to Cambodia in dealing with EU's revocation of EBA. During the goodwill visit of Prime Minister Hun Sen to Beijing on 6th February 2020 to shore up support and solidarity with Chinese people amidst the outbreak of Covid-19 coronavirus, President Xi Jinping reaffirmed China's support for Cambodia in the face of EU's pressures. He reportedly said, "I know Cambodia is being pressured by the European Union over EBA. No matter what, Cambodia should not bow to the EU."[12]

In February 2020, the European Commission decided to partially withdraw Cambodia's preferential access to the EU market under EBA due to "the serious and systematic violations of the human rights principles enshrined in the International Covenant on Civil and Political Rights". This partial removal will affect around 20 percent or €1 billion of Cambodia's yearly exports to the EU including garment products, footwear, travel goods and sugar.[13]

The EU is pressing Cambodia to "re-open the political space in the country, to create the necessary conditions for the re-establishment of a credible, democratic opposition and to initiate a democratic process of national reconciliation through genuine and inclusive dialogue". It also wanted Cambodia to reinstate political rights of the opposition members and revise laws, such as the Law on Political Parties and the Law on Non-governmental Organisations.[14]

---

[11] Sun Mesa, "Prime Minister vows to hit back if EU revokes EBA trade status", Khmer Times, 11 February 2020, available at https://www.khmertimeskh.com/50689696/prime-minister-vows-to-hit-back-if-eu-revokes-eba-trade-status

[12] Sun Mesa, "China will support Kingdom despite EBA withdrawal: Official", Khmer Times, 7 February 2020, https://www.khmertimeskh.com/50688230/china-will-support-kingdom-despite-eba-withdrawal-official

[13] European Commission, Trade/Human Rights: Commission decides to partially withdraw Cambodia's preferential access to the EU market. https://ec.europa.eu/commission/presscorner/detail/en/ip_20_229

[14] European Commission, Trade/Human Rights: Commission decides to partially withdraw Cambodia's preferential access to the EU market. https://ec.europa.eu/commission/presscorner/detail/en/ip_20_229

In response, Prime Minister Hun Sen accused the EU of applying "double standard" when it comes to political development, and sees the EU's measure as a violation of national sovereignty, and interference into Cambodia's judicial system. However, the statement of the Ministry of Foreign Affairs and International Cooperation keeps the door open for more dialogue and future bilateral engagement. It reads, "Notwithstanding the EC's decision on this trade matter, Cambodia remains firmly committed to further enhancing its relations with the European Union on the spirit of mutual respect and interest all the while reaffirming its full aspiration to remain within the region a multiparty liberal democracy".[15]

Conclusion

The EU has played an important role in socio-economic development and poverty reduction in Cambodia. However, there are real differences and tensions over the issue of human rights and democracy. Cambodia regards the EU's selective normative approach to small states as "double standard" and the act of violating Cambodia's independence and sovereignty. Using EBA trade preferential treatment as a tool to put pressures and conditions on Cambodia is seen as counterproductive as Cambodia, unlike during the 1990s and 2000s, has more strategic choices and hence more willing to resist external pressures on human rights and democracy. The EU needs to understand the usefulness and effectiveness of its economic sanctions or punishments in dealing with other countries. On its part, Cambodia needs to continue the dialogue with the EU and to improve its democracy and open up space for civil society and trade unions not as a "favour" to the EU but to sustain its own long-term peace and economic development in a socially inclusive framework.

---

[15] Ministry of Foreign Affairs and International Cooperation of Cambodia, Statement on the Decision of the European Commission on Tariffs Preferences under the EBA regime. 12 February 2020.

10

Indonesia-EU Relations
Close Partners or Distant Associates?

Evi Fitriani

Indonesia's relationship with the European Union (EU) is not always in a good shape despite diplomatic rhetoric from both sides that they share common values and close cooperation. How close is this bilateral relationship compared to EU's relations with other ASEAN member states? Given the fact that Indonesia is Southeast Asian biggest economy and largest market with 260 million population, the country came only the sixth in line on EU's bilateral FTA agenda, after negotiations were launched with Singapore, Malaysia, Vietnam, Thailand, and the Philippines. This gave the perception to some Indonesians that Indonesia is not a top priority for the EU when dealing with Southeast Asia. Similarly, Indonesia has perceived the EU as a distant partner. This essay explains the problems that complicate Indonesia-EU relations and put forward some perspectives on future relations of the two parties.

Not All Smooth-sailing

Indonesia's relations with the EU has not been all smooth-sailing. There has been several problematic issues between the two. Over time, some of these problems were resolved due to the changes within Indonesian society itself, but some have persisted and new issues emerged.

To begin with, human rights and the pace and progress of democratization were two sensitive political issues that hindered Indonesia's relations with the EU in the 1980s and 1990s. The EU was perceived as a constant "intruder" into Indonesia domestic politics during President Suharto authoritarian regime. Indonesians were not convinced that European criticism on human rights and democratic practices in Indonesia was simply value-driven. Instead some Indonesians believed that human rights issues were used as a bargaining tool to achieve European economic interests. Indonesian critics of the EU often referred to the historical exploitation by Europeans during the colonial period to question European's credibility to talk about human rights.

After the fall of Suharto, Indonesia went through a chaotic and complex process of democratization. Despite many difficulties and setbacks, Indonesia has proven it could embrace democracy and, since 2004, has successfully held the most complicated multi-level direct elections in the world. As Indonesia democratizes Indonesia and EU seem to have tone down their debates on human rights. Indonesia has become more confident to discuss human rights issues especially after observing that the EU has struggled to live up to their own commitment to human rights when dealing with refugees and Muslim migrants.

However as the tensions over human rights and democratization subside, new problems related to Indonesia's environmental practices and its palm oil industries have emerged.

Under EU pressure, Indonesia voluntarily entered a partnership agreement with the EU to fight illegal logging through Forest Law Enforcement, Governance and Trade (FLEGT) license in 2016 in order to comply with the EU strict environmental standard. Indonesia and EU have also cooperated in various climate change initiatives and other similar programs. However, in recent years Indonesians perceived that environmental issues have been used as a non-tarrif barrier to protect the economic interests of particular agriculture presure groups in several EU countries. This raised the question if EU's commitment to fair and open trading system is just an empty slogan.

Beyond such specific issues as human rights and environmental protectionism, Indonesia-EU relations also suffers from a deficiency in trust due to the perceptions of how Indonesia was unfairly treated during the Asian Financial crisis (AFC). Many Indonesians still remembered how Western countries pushed the country into socio-economic difficulties through devastating structural adjustment imposed by the World Bank and the International Monetary Fund during the AFC. In the WTO, Indonesian and other developing countries often had to contend with agenda set and norms imposed by developed countries and the EU which negotiates on behalf of its member states.

In early 2000s Indonesia was also sanctioned by the European and other Western countries on the country's defense procurements. Indonesia was banned on arms purchasing, including on importing spare-parts for jet-fighters that the country had bought from the US and European countries. It created a crisis in Indonesian defense system and undermined Indonesian role as a key country to maintain stability and security in the region. Such bitter memories encouraged Indonesia to find alternative major partners.

The trust deficit in Indonesia and the EU meant the two are more like distant partners rather than natural partners. The fact that the EU does not always act in unity and competes with its own member states in its diplomatic presence in Indonesia puts further obstacles in strengthening relations at the EU-Indonesia level. Indonesia enjoys good relations with several EU member states such as the Netherlands and Germany. Developing the bilateral relations with these EU member states seem to be preferable approach by Indonesia to develop mutual understandings and deepen cooperation.

Some Positive Developments in Recent Years

Despite the obstacles in Indonesia-EU relations as discussed above, the two have been able to establish formal bilateral mechanism to further cooperation after the signing of the Partnership and Cooperation Agreement (PCA). The PCA entered into force in May 2014 and since then has facilitated dialogue from security to human rights, including a High Level Dialogue on Maritime and Fisheries. There is also cooperation in inter-faith dialogue and some talks to cooperate in education, research and technology but the latter are not as robust as expected.

More importantly, Indonesia and the EU have begun negotiations for a comprehensive economic partnership agreement (CEPA) since 2016. The ninth round of the negotiation took place in December 2019 despite heightening tensions over the proposed ban on import of palm oil for biofuel in the EU. Insights from the meetings revealed difficulties in the negotiation as EU had strived to keep Indonesia as source of raw materials rather than accepting the latter's processed or semi-finished export products. There is still no clue as to when the CEPA negotiation will conclude as Indonesia needs to be mindful of the scrutiny by its parliament and non-governmental organisations. The example from the Republic of Korea that has suffered trade deficits after signing the FTA with the EU in 2012 also offered some lessons and warning for the Indonesians to be cautious in its negotiations with the EU.

It is undeniable that current developments in Indonesia-EU relations are driven by economic imperatives. It is general knowledge that economic interests are paramount in the EU's approach to Asian countries in general and Southeast Asian countries in particular. Even though the EU launched "a new" strategy in 2015 to upgrade relations with Southeast Asia to one with a strategic purpose, economics still dominate. Seen from the Indonesian perspective, the "strategic purpose" of the EU is aimed at protecting long-term access to raw materials, market and investment in the region. For some Indonesians, such predominantly materialistic motive can be problematic as they wonder what would happen when the economic incentives disappeared. This phenomenon is quite noticeable when Asian countries including Indonesia were torn by the Asian financial crisis. The EU only returned to the region after the regional countries regained their economic strengths a decade after the crisis. This led to questions in the minds of some Indonesia if the EU is only a fair weather friend.

For some Indonesians, this pragmatic approach to interactions is inherently unstable and this kind of relations cannot be categorized as a partnership, let alone a strategic partnership. It is too transactional. Instead a partnership must be based on a more idealistic motivation. When Indonesian and EU leaders signed the PCA on 26 April 2014, this is only the first step towards building a real partnership. Much more need to be done before the two become real partners.

More Focus on Trust Building

There are several areas that Indonesia and EU can develop for a more comprehensive and less materialistic relations. Challenging geopolitics in East Asia and world's contemporary gloomy picture should drive the two to work together. Indonesian and EU leaders declared at the end of their official meeting recently that the two would cooperate in addressing regional and global issues of mutual interest. This include in particular cooperation on migration issues, human rights and legal affairs, countering the proliferation of weapons of mass destruction, combating terrorism and transnational crimes, raising the profiles of both Parties in each other's regions, and promoting people-to-people understanding. In functional cooperation, there are three other areas that can also be included: marine conservation and maritime security, forest fire and water resources management.

Apart from the functional cooperation, education and people-to-people interactions are vital for trust building. Cooperation in higher education that include research collaboration to develop science and technology, and to build workable multi-cultural societies are needed both by Indonesia and EU countries nowadays. This kind of cooperation should include a wide range of stake holders. Relations between Indonesia and EU are too complex and too rich to be handled only by government officials and business communities. Involvement of other non-state actors can help nurture a wider base and deeper foundation for a partnership. In addition, collaborative education in socio-cultural matters can encourage long term trust building and enrich people to people ties. It will take time and resources from both sides but it eventually can result in stronger foundation for a long term sustainable partnership important also in strategic and economic field. Both Indonesia and EU need to invest more in educational cooperation if they are serious in building long term partnerships.

The trust building is needed not only between Indonesia and EU but also between EU and other ASEAN countris as Indonesia is not the only one with the trust deficit toward EU. Because of different histories, each ASEAN countries has different level of relations and engagements with EU and its member states. In fact, despite its support to ASEAN integration, EU bilateral approach towards FTA with individual ASEAN member states may deepen the economic gap across ASEAN member countries as the rich gets richer and the poors are left behind. The EU thus needs to be more aware of possible contradictions between its regional and bilateral priorities.

11

Laos-EU Relations
A Laos Perspective

Sayakane Sisouvong

Introduction

The first European arrived in the Kingdom of Lao Lan Xang[1] nearly four centuries ago. Today, not only citizens from all European countries have visited the Lao People's Democratic Republic (Lao PDR or Laos), but Laos has also established diplomatic relations with all European countries. Formal diplomatic relations with the European Union (EU, then the European Community or EC) was established on 21 November 1975. Europeans, Americans and others recognize Laos' geostrategic location and abundant natural resources, but have yet to tap Laos' great potential.

Laos has strong determination to extend its hands of friendship and achieve cooperation for mutual benefit with all its neighbours and countries around the world regardless of their political systems. It has established diplomatic relations with 143 countries and with the European Union and became a member of ASEAN in 1997.

---

[1] The Lan Xang Kingdom was named by the French colonizer in late 19th century as 'Laos'. In 1975 the Kingdom became the Lao People's Democratic Republic. Currently, it is also acceptable to call 'Laos' or 'Lao PDR' as a shorter version of the Lao People's Democratic Republic.

This essay focuses on Laos- EU relations throughout four and a half decades of their diplomatic relations.

Laos and Europe: Time-honoured Bond of Friendship

The Lao and European peoples have built and nurtured a strong foundation of relationship centuries ago. The first few Europeans who visited the Lao Lan Xang Kingdom, Mr. Gerrot Van Wuysthoff, a Dutch merchant in 1641–42 and an Italian Jesuit missionary, G.M. Leris, between 1642–48, described the Lao Kingdom, during their visits, as having considerable riches and power, the splendor of the royal court and the religious ceremonies.[2] Then there was already a good recognition of the vast peaceful, prosperous and powerful landlocked Lao Kingdom[3] with its geo-strategic location and abundant natural resources.

In November 2020, Laos and the EU will celebrate the 45th Anniversary of the establishment of their diplomatic relations.

Laos and EU established diplomatic relations in 1975 at the end of the Indochina War. Then, the Cold War had still not ended, but both managed to steer their relationships towards mutual benefit in the Cold War environment. Despite their differences, Laos and the EU have steadily improved their bilateral relations. Initially, the EU appointed its Delegation in Bangkok to accredit to Laos. In 2003 the EU opened its Mission in Vientiane at Charge d'Affaires level and in September 2016 the European Union upgraded its Delegation to a full-fledged Diplomatic Mission. For its part, Laos initially appointed its Ambassador in Paris to accredit to the EU. In 1998 Lao Government opened its Mission in Brussels to directly handle the growing ties between them. The elevation of Laos and the EU representations to ambassadorial level mark a new era in their bilateral relations.

---

[2] *Ancient Luang Prabang & Laos*, by Denise Heywood, page 18 (edition of 2014).

[3] Then the size of the Lao Kingdom was double the current one which is 236,800 km^2.

Laos' and the EU's unique and fruitful bilateral relations are characterized by the following points:

Firstly, although Laos is a socialist country run by one political party, it has a market oriented economy and welcomes investments from the EU and all corners of the world.

Secondly, Laos is a proud member state of the Association of Southeast Asian Nations (ASEAN) and is its only landlocked country. ASEAN is not a supranational regional organisation like the EU. ASEAN embraces diversity and welcome member states with different political systems and at different levels of economic development. ASEAN adheres to the principles of non-interference, sovereign equality and consensus. Despite all these, Laos is keen to learn from the EU, for example on how it provides assistance to new member states which are former socialist countries to integrate into the mainstream of EU. The EU's successful experiences and lessons of connectivity between and among landlocked EU member states is of interest to Laos as well.

Thirdly, Laos like the member states of the EU has gone through the horrors of devastating wars. Both realize how precious peace and development cooperation are. ASEAN and the EU have been established to prevent wars and focus on cooperation for the well being of the peoples of ASEAN and the EU and beyond.

Fourthly, despite the disparities in economic development, Laos can be an important partner for the EU. Laos' domestic political stability is important in contributing to the maintenance of regional peace and stability. Laos' geostrategic location, serving as a gate way to and from China, has become all the more important and certainly will bring more benefits to ASEAN, China and the EU. The shortest and most economical route of the Singapore-Kunming Rail Link (SKRL) through Laos which will be completed by the end of 2021 is a good example. This project will also help realize the Master Plan on ASEAN Connectivity

2025. Once completed, this project will be the first ever rail link between ASEAN and the EU. Without Laos' decision to seek funding and technical support from China, the SKRL which was first proposed by ASEAN in 1995 during the ASEAN Mekong Basin Development Cooperation (AMBDC) Summit more than two decades ago would have not been realized. In addition to existing air links, highway link through Laos to Kunming is now under construction.

Fifthly, while Laos and EU share similar goals on peace and development, there are also different interests. Because of different historical backgrounds, cultures, religions and levels of socio-economic development, their priorities differed. Laos, for instance, seek the right to development and have a better quality of life, highly appreciates the United Nations for the existing MDGs' set of 8 measurable goals,[4] but also the inclusion of the Goal 9: Reduce impact of UXO (unexploded ordinances), that is the legacy of the Indochina war.

The above-mentioned differences and specificities have led Laos to have different perceptions and approaches, for example on human rights. However, Laos and the EU have also decided to put aside some of these differences to seek a new era of bilateral relations which will bring more mutual benefits through carrying out many areas of cooperation.

Laos-EU Cooperation

Laos-EU Cooperation Agreement of 1997 is in line with the EU's new strategy for Asia and the ASEAN countries.[5] The EU has a strategic interest in supporting Asia's regional integration, and

---

[4] The MDGs' 8 goals are: 1. Eradicate Extreme Poverty and Hunger, 2. Achieve Universal Primary Education, 3. Promote Gender Equality ad Empower Women, 4. Reduce Child Mortality, 5. Improve Maternal Health, 6. Combat HIV/AIDS, Malaria and other diseases, 7. Ensure Environmental Sustainability, and 8. A Global Partnership for Development.

[5] Stavros Papagianneas, Managing Director of StP Communications and author of *Re-branding Europe* (28 Jan. 2019).

pursues partnership and cooperation agreements (PCAs) with individual ASEAN member countries.

The EU works closely with Lao government to identify areas of cooperation that are in line with Laos' socio-economic development plans. Currently, the EU is supporting the Lao Eighth National Socio-Economic Development Plan (2016–2020) which focuses on achieving high economic growth. The EU 2014–2020 programme for Laos focuses on nutrition, education and governance, while also tackling issues such as UXO decontamination, gender equality and climate change.

In June 2016 the EU Joint Programming in Laos entitled the "European Joint Programming document for Lao People's Democratic Republic 2016–2020" was adopted. This document laid the foundations for European partners to join forces to provide a response that was well coordinated with other development partners' support to Laos.[6] This document is also aligned with Laos' national development strategy by using the 8th National Socio-Economic Development Plan (NSEDP) timetable, pursuing goals included in the NSEDP and promoting the use of government reporting, monitoring and evaluation. It is also the foundation for dialogue on fundamental human rights, environmental protection and the expansion of good governance practices in Laos.

European partners have jointly identified seven 'priority sectors' in which they have a comparative advantage. These include Agriculture and Rural Development, Education, Environment and Natural Resources, Governance, Health, Nutrition and Private Sector Development, including Technical, Vocational Education and Training and Tourism. The joint support of the European partners also focuses on the development of the economy, especially value chains, trade and investment policy in the context of the ASEAN Economic Community (AEC).

---

[6] European partners (comprising the EU, Finland, France, Germany, Hungary, Ireland, Luxembourg, the United Kingdom and Switzerland).

The sectors are aligned with the Lao government's policies. Coordination is ensured through the relevant working group mechanism, thus enabling ownership. European partners are harmonising their programmes through this joint programming exercise with each sector contributing to a results framework linked to monitoring indicators included in the 8th NSEDP to enable mutual accountability for results.

In addition to the priority sectors, European partners are also committed to providing significant financial and technical support in complementary sectors and on cross-cutting policy priorities.[7]

To oversee overall Laos-EU cooperation and its implementation, Laos and the EU established a Joint Committee in 2003 with three working groups (WG): WG on Trade, WG on Cooperation and WG on Human Rights Dialogue. The Joint Committee, with its three working groups, is an important mechanism to help deepen mutual understanding and forge closer ties between Laos and the EU.

Recommendations for a New Era of Laos-EU Friendship

Looking to the 45 years of bilateral relations, Laos and the EU are now ready to move their cooperation to a higher plane with better understanding and appreciation of each other's specificities and respect for each other's self-determination. At the same time, the world has also changed beyond imagination. The following are recommendations for better Laos-EU cooperation:

---

[7] **Cross-cutting issues** — protection of fundamental human rights, gender equality, protection and inclusion of disadvantaged minorities, democratic governance and combating corruption, sustainable environmental management and climate change mitigation and adaptation, resettlement practices on a voluntary basis. **Complementary sectors** — support to civil society, climate finance, culture and heritage, disaster risk reduction/preparedness, democracy and human rights, lending from the European Investment Bank, energy, investment, support to the Mekong River Commission, migration, multilateral institutions, regional integration, research and innovation, scholarships and higher education, statistics, youth and un-exploded ordinances.

At regional / sub-regional level:

1. The EU is behind some of ASEAN's major dialogue partners in setting up mechanisms to cooperate with the new ASEAN Member States — Cambodia, Laos, Myanmar and Vietnam (CLMV) and the Mekong riparian states. For example, Japan is active in the Greater Mekong Sub-region (GMS, Japan), China in the Lancang-Mekong Cooperation (LMC, China), US with the Lower Mekong Initiative (LMI, USA) and India with the Mekong-Ganga Cooperation (India) amongst others. It is recommended that the EU act soon to propose a new mechanism for cooperation between the CLMV countries and the EU.

2. A mechanism among CLMV-China-EU to promote cooperation in areas under connectivity, especially after the completion of the SKRL through Laos.

3. A new platform to promote ASEAN-China-EU cooperation with respect to the Belt and Road Initiative of China.

At national level:

1. While appreciating the EU and its member states for their support to Laos in the implementation of its Socio-Economic Development Plan, it is recommended that the EU works closely with Laos to identify new sectors of cooperation to enable Laos to respond timely to the fast changing world.

2. Laos needs more assistance in the sector of education, capacity building and transfer of technology. The more educated and skilled the Lao people, the greater benefits it will bring to Laos and the EU and beyond.

3. Trade and investment are very important to Laos and the EU. Being a member of ASEAN and the WTO, Laos is in support of EU's multilateralism. Laos also highly appreciates the EU for extending its Generalised Scheme of Preferences (GSP),

namely the Everything-But-Arms (EBA) scheme to Laos. However, taking the 2018 statistics into consideration, two way trade volume of 408 million Euros between Laos and the EU reflects the need to redouble efforts to address pending challenges. The EU should encourage more investments into Laos bringing EU standard and relevant technology to ensure products make in Laos meet all EU's rules and regulations.

4. Laos and the EU have two different political systems. However, despite differences, a more robust foundation has been built after forty-five years of their fruitful cooperation. The two should not allow any issues, like human rights, to derail their broader and greater strategic interest.

5. To some observers, the UK's exit may mean a sign of weakness inside the EU and Covid-19 may bring about untold loss of human lives and devastating impact on the economies of the EU. Despite these challenges, the EU, being the most successful regional organisation, should not retreat from ASEAN, including Laos. Instead the EU should step up engagement and move quickly to realise some of the opportunities in ASEAN.

Conclusion

Laos and the EU have successfully steered forward their bilateral relations in the last four decades and a half, despite their different political systems and the fast changing international arena.

For its part, Laos has taken unprecedented major steps to gradually transform from a landlocked developing socialist country into an important land-link and gate way to and from China. Laos surrounded by five neighbours (China, Vietnam, Cambodia, Thailand and Myanmar) with their combined population of nearly 1.5 billion people offers great business opportunities. Moreover, the shortest and most economical route of the Singapore-Kunming Rail Link (SKRL) through Laos, which will be completed in December 2021, provides ample proof that it will be the most direct land route to Europe, opening up new business opportunities. A regional hub is coming into being as dry ports, highway link between Vientiane and Kunming and other facilities are now being built in tandem with the SKRL.

Apart from being a responsible member of the UN and many UN Agencies, Laos has launched its New Economic Mechanism (NEM), an outward looking market-oriented policy and became a full member of ASEAN (1997), having the ASEAN Economic Community (AEC) as an important pillar, and a member of the WTO (2013). These are all rule-based organisations in which Laos fully subscribes to. However, Laos need further assistance in building its capacity and with cooperation with the EU, Laos will be able to fully integrate into the mainstream of ASEAN and the global economy.

From now onwards, Laos' enormous potential combined with the EU's great achievements and tremendous strength will create more opportunities and greater benefits to ASEAN, East Asia, Europe and beyond.

However, the above-mentioned potential benefits will not be realised if the EU should decide to retreat using Covid-19, Brexit and other challenges as its excuse. ASEAN and European citizen and others will closely follow Brussels' action in weeks and months ahead. The EU should increase its presence in Laos and in ASEAN commensurate to its size and power, and continue to promote multilateralism.

12

Malaysia-EU Relations
Themes and Evolution

Nur Shahadah Jamil

Introduction

Malaysia-EU relations are rooted in the broader Malaysia-Europe relations. Its manifestations have been multi-faceted, multi-layered and dynamic. The evolution and prospects of Malaysia-EU relations are a function of three factors, namely historical legacy, institutional dynamics, and the primacy of economics; each of which is filtered and determined by the Malaysian ruling elites' domestic political interests. These themes help explain the main characteristics and limitations of Malaysia-EU relations, and show that the relations are more than just a relationship between a sovereign country and a regional body. Rather, it is a complex, evolving process that has been, and will continue to be coloured and conditioned by the governing elites' domestic considerations, bilateral linkages, and multilateral interactions.

Through the discussion of the three themes, one can observe the evolution in Malaysia-EU relations since Malaya first obtained its independence from the British in 1957 until the era of Mahathir Administration 2.0. The shift, however, is not an indication that Malaysia has abandoned its cooperation nor adjusted its overall foreign policy with the EU. In fact, such shift is driven very much by both external and domestic considerations. Externally, like other smaller states in the region, Malaysia needs to deal with the uncertainties in the evolving international environment. Domestically, Malaysian political elites need to ensure their regime survival by constantly attempting to maintain and strengthen their regime legitimation, particularly in terms of performance legitimation via the country's economic growth.

Theme I: Historical Legacy

Malaysia-EU relations are rooted in its relations with different European states in the earlier stages. When Malaya gained its independence from the British in 1957, a huge part of its relations with Europe was with Britain — its former colonial power. However, this did not mean that Malaysia neglected its relations with other European states. Malaysia also established relations with several countries of Western Europe such as France, Germany and Netherlands.

There are several factors that can explain Malaysia's close relations with Britain during this period of time. These factors can be clustered into defence and security, as well as economic dependency. Communist insurgency at home was the number one threat of the Malaysian Government at that time before it eventually ended in 1989 with the signing of a Peace Treaty between the Malaysian Government and Communist Party of Malaya. Meanwhile, this period also witnessed the emergence of conflict between Malaysia and Indonesia when the latter launched the *"Konfrontasi"* against Malaya in opposing the formation of Malaysia in 1963. To manage these challenges and ensure its survival, Malaysia in its early years of independence had no choice but to rely on other powers, particularly Britain for its defence and security. Hence, Malaysia became a member of several multilateral defence arrangements with Britain such as the Anglo-Malayan Defence Agreement (AMDA) since 1957 and the Five Power Defence Arrangement (FPDA) since 1970.

In addition, Malaysia also heavily relied on the British in terms of economic development and trade. This is because during British rule, the colonial authority has adopted a *laissez faire* economic system which allowed the British to remain as the dominant economic force in the country even more than a decade after Malaysia gained its independence in 1957. Furthermore, the economy of Malaysia at that time depended mainly on the export of raw materials, namely tin and natural rubber. Exports of raw material were subjected to many uncertainties and hence price volatility. For example, the price of natural rubber went on a downslide due to competition from synthetic rubber. As a result, efforts to diversify production and income away from tin and rubber began to gain the attention of Malaysian political elites since late 1960s.

A sharp change of policy can be observed with the resignation on Tunku Abdul Rahman as Prime Minister of Malaysia in 1970. His successor — Tun Abdul Razak Hussein took office and re-oriented the country's foreign policy from pro-Western and anti-Communist to a policy of Non-Alignment. Several reasons contributed to the policy change — this include the withdrawal of British forces from bases in both Malaysia and Singapore, as well as the reduction of U.S ground troops in Southeast Asia as enunciated by President Nixon's Guam Doctrine in July 1969.[1] Realising that they could not count on Britain and the West as security provider, Malaysian leaders started to focus more on self-reliance and regionalism.

In the economic sphere, re-orientation away from the West could be traced during Tun Mahathir's first term as the Prime Minister of Malaysia. He launched the "Buy British Last" campaign in the early months of his administration and restructured the nation's economy through large scale diversification programs to change the direction and composition of exports

---

[1] Kuik Cheng-Chwee, "Analyzing Malaysian's Changing Alignment Choices, 1971–89," *Jebat: Malaysian Journal of History, Politics and Strategic Studies*, Vol.37, (2010), p.32.

from rubber to oil palm (and other crops), as well as from primary to secondary industries (especially manufacturing). As a result of such historical legacy, while Malaysia-Europe relations continue to progress today, its relations with Europe is still very much dominated by bilateral ties with individual European states.

Theme II: Institutional Dynamics

The era of 1970s witnessed how a multi-layered Malaysia-Europe relations began to emerge through the institutionalization of Malaysia-EU relations via the Association of Southeast Asian Nation (ASEAN). The EU became a formal dialogue partner of ASEAN in 1977, and expanded its cooperation with ASEAN through participation in the ASEAN Regional Forum (ARF) and the Asia-Europe Meeting (ASEM). Malaysia, in the early years of its independence did not have a strong influence in the international arena. Therefore, regionalism was a perfect option to strengthen its bargaining power. Alongside with other Southeast Asian states through ASEAN, it subsequently benefited from various ASEAN-EU initiatives.

On 7 March 1980, the Cooperation Agreement between ASEAN and the European Community was signed in Kuala Lumpur. The agreement aimed to demonstrate common will among signatories to enter a new phase of economic and development cooperation. However, until the late 1980s, ASEAN remained still situated at the bottom of EC's hierarchy of relations, below even those of African, Latin American and Caribbean's states.[2] In the 1990s, development of ASEAN-EU relations was hampered by human right issues.

With the pragmatic turn by the EU to engage Southeast Asia not only at a region-to-region level, but also with individual

---

[2] Yeo Lay Hwee, *Asia and Europe: The Development and Different Dimensions of ASEM* (London: Routledge, 2003), p.21.

ASEAN member states, relationship between Malaysia and the EU began to take off. This was reflected in the establishment of the European Commission Delegation Office in Kuala Lumpur in 2003. Another notable progress in the relations was the launch of negotiations for a Partnership and Cooperation Agreement (PCA) and a Free Trade Agreement (FTA) by the then Prime Minister of Malaysia, Najib Tun Razak, and the President of European Commission, Jose Manuel Barroso in October 5, 2010. Both initiatives aimed not only at boosting bilateral trade and investment, but also to create new strategic dimension for Malaysia-EU political dialogue and economic cooperation. Negotiations for the PCA were concluded on December 8, 2015 after 11 rounds of negotiations, while those for FTA are on hold due to various reasons since 2012.[3]

Exchanges and cooperation in the social and cultural arenas also flourished during this era, especially through various programs stemming from the Asia-Europe Meeting (ASEM) initiatives. Under the political pillar of ASEM initiatives, Malaysia benefitted from several environmental and human rights programmes such as the Asia Pro Econ 11 programme. At the same time, under the economic and finance pillar, Malaysia was involved in programmes including the Asia-Invest II and EC ASEAN Intellectual Property Program II (ECAP II), while under the socio-cultural and intellectual pillar which focuses on education and research, Malaysia benefitted from programmes such as Asia-Link, the ASEAN-EC University Network and Erasmus Mundus Scholarships program.

Theme III: The Primacy of Economics

The most important factor in shaping Malaysia-EU relations, especially in the post-Cold War era, is economics. Bilateral trade

---

[3] See official web site of Malaysia's Ministry of International Trade and Industry, https://fta.miti.gov.my/index.php/pages/view/meufta, accessed on 5 February 2020.

between Malaysia and the EU totalled €39.3 billion in 2018.[4] The EU is the third largest trading partner of Malaysia after China and Singapore, accounting for more than 10% of Malaysia's total trade, while Malaysia is the EU's 23rd largest trading partner in goods for the same period.[5] Although Malaysia is not a major trading partner in services, the level of trade in services has also experienced substantial growth of 59% for the period of 2009–2015. The EU is also one of the largest investor in Malaysia, primarily in manufacturing and increasingly in the services sector. Trade volume with the EU grew 17.5 per cent in 2017 in comparison with 2016 and with robust export growth notably with Germany and the Netherlands.[6]

However, in 2018, Malaysia-EU relations hit a rocky patch over the palm oil issue. The EU is the second largest importer of Malaysia palm oil after India, buying 12% of total palm oil produced by Malaysia in 2018. When the European Commission concluded in early 2019 that palm oil cultivation has resulted in deforestation of rainforest in Southeast Asia and therefore its use as bio-fuel should be phased out in the EU by 2030, Malaysia, as the world's second largest palm oil producer after Indonesia, has refuted the claims and called it misleading. The EU's resolution on palm oil is economically detrimental to the industry, especially to some 650,000 oil palm smallholders in the country.[7]

Mahathir, who came back to power as the 7th prime minister in 2018, during an interview in March 2019 warned the EU that it

---

[4] See official web site of the European Commission, https://ec.europa.eu/trade/policy/countries-and-regions/countries/malaysia/, accessed on 7 February 2020.

[5] Ibid.

[6] See official web site of Malaysia External Trade Development Corporation, http://www.matrade.gov.my/en/for-foreign-buyers/industry-capabilities/trade-statistics/158-malaysian-exporters/trade-performance-2017, accessed on 7 February 2020.

[7] "EU-Malaysia Ties to Remain Strong Despite Palm Oil Issue, Says EU Ambassador," 12 May 2019, The Star Online, https://www.thestar.com.my/news/nation/2019/05/12/eu-msia-ties-to-remain-strong-despite-palm-oil-issue-says-eu-ambassador, accessed on 20 January 2020.

risked starting a trade war with Malaysia over its "grossly unfair" policies. Malaysia cast the EU's restrictions against palm oil as a protectionist measure to protect other alternatives such as rapeseed oil that Europe produces.[8] Malaysia has since raised its concerns over EU's palm oil restriction at several World Trade Organization (WTO) meetings including the Committee on Trade in Environment (CTE) on 5 May 2019; Technical Barriers to Trade (TBT) on 20-21 June 2019; as well as Council on Trade in Goods (CTG) on 8-9 July 2019.[9] The Ministry also urged the EU to accept and recognize the certification scheme and expressed the Government's commitment to negotiate with the EU in a sincere and constructive manner over the issue.[10]

The Malaysian Government tries to convince the EU that the cultivation of palm oil does not cause environmental problems as they claimed. The Malaysian oil palm industry is committed to produce palm oil in accordance with the Malaysian Sustainable Palm Oil (MSPO) Certification Scheme, which has been implemented on a mandatory basis since December 2019.[11] The Ministry of Primary Industries has also committed to planting one million forest tree species within the next few years particularly in degraded forest land in Sabah sponsored mainly by oil palm industry players.[12] The Ministry has also donated RM1.5

---

[8] A. Anathalakshmi, Joseph Sipalan and Joe Brock, "Exclusive: EU Risks 'Trade War' with Malaysia over Palm Oil — Mahathir," 28 March 2019, *Reuters*, https://www.reuters.com/article/us-malaysia-politics-mahathir-exclusive/exclusive-eu-risks-trade-war-with-malaysia-over-palm-oil-mahathir-idUSKCN1R917W, accessed on 15 January 2020.

[9] *"Media Statement: Palm Oil Issues with European Union (EU),"* Ministry of International Trade and Industry of Malaysia, released on 29 July 2019.

[10] "Malaysia Urges EU to Recognize MSPO Certification," 29 July 2019, *New Straits Times*, https://www.nst.com.my/news/nation/2019/07/508316/malaysia-urges-eu-recognise-mspo-certification, accessed on 2 February 2020.

[11] Ibid.

[12] Muguntan Vanar, "Federal Government to Help Wildlife Conservation and Reforestation Efforts in Sabah," 2 April 2019, *The Star Online*, https://www.thestar.com.my/news/nation/2019/04/02/federal-government-to-help-wildlife-conservation-and-reforestation-efforts-in-sabah/, accessed on 2 February 2020.

million to the Sabah Wildlife Department to boost orang utan and elephant conservation efforts.[13]

Malaysia has yet to file a lawsuit to the WTO like what Jakarta did on 15 December 2019. However, there is a high possibility that the Malaysian government will do the same within the next few months. In fact, it is also very likely that Malaysia might not ratify the PCA which has been concluded in 2015 and will not resume FTA negotiations with the EU until the issue of such unfair and discriminatory practices against palm oil is resolved. Thus, it would be fair to say that Malaysia-EU relation under Mahathir 2.0 is heavily influenced and dented by the palm oil agenda.

This comes as no surprise because palm oil and palm-based products are currently Malaysia's fifth major export commodity generating RM62.7 billion in earnings for the first 11 months in 2018.[14] With overall production of 39% of global output, the palm oil industry has contributed to 37.9% of the GDP of agriculture sector in 2018 or approximately 2.8% of total GDP of the country. Thus, disruption in palm oil export will be quite a heavy blow to the Malaysian economy and the welfare of more than three million people whose livelihood depends on and along the supply chain. Therefore, the current administration must be vocal about the ban in order to ensure the legitimacy of the newly formed government by maintaining the same level of economic growth in the country (if not further boost it), to avoid comparison from being made with the previous leadership. This is also in line with Mahathir's usual stance against unfair treatment of major powers towards smaller states in international dealings.

---

[13] Ibid.

[14] "Palm Oil to Remain Malaysia's Major Export Despite Challenges: PM," 19 November 2019, *Xinhuanet*, http://www.xinhuanet.com/english/2019-11/19/c_138566473.htm, accessed on 3 February 2020.

Conclusion

To conclude, Malaysia-EU relation is unique in a sense that it is multi-layered, multi-faceted and dynamic. Shaped by three different themes filtered by domestic considerations of Malaysian ruling elites, the relation has also evolved across time: from pro-Western and anti-Communist to a policy of non-alignment; from bilateral interactions to a mix of bilateral and multilateral engagement; and shift of focus in the relationship from mainly defence and security to more of economic development and socio-cultural collaboration. Each of the three themes influenced Malaysia-EU relations differently at different times and the most important theme shaping the relationship particularly in the post-Cold War era would be the primacy of the economy. This is most evident in the way the issue over palm oil has clouded the bilateral ties. Thus, in order for Malaysia-EU relations to continue to progress as desired, the first thing both party need to do is to work towards solving the issue before it does more damage to the relationship.

13

Myanmar, ASEAN and EU
Finding the Nexus

Moe Thuzar

In 2016, Myanmar seemed set on transforming its authoritarian past to a democracy under a civilian government that had been elected via a landslide of support across the country. Four years later, Myanmar faces accusations of crimes against humanity at the International Court of Justice (ICJ) which has voiced its concern on the potential threat of these crimes sliding towards genocide. International criticism now besets the National League for Democracy (NLD) government in a sad parallel to those levelled against the military regime (which ruled Myanmar from 1988 to 2010) that had suppressed the NLD's democracy movement. Indeed, post-2016 Myanmar's relations with the West — once critics of the military junta suppressing the NLD — seem to have come full circle, with Myanmar's foreign relations taking an Asian turn with an ASEAN focus.

However, there is recognition that 'piling on' Myanmar may be counterproductive. The European Union (EU)'s approach to its interactions with Myanmar takes this into account. As the EU's policy towards Myanmar is focused on assisting the country in its transition, the current situation in Myanmar requires the EU to structure its generous assistance for this transition process towards healing deep ethnic and socio-economic divides in the country. The EU's programmes in Myanmar can provide additional avenues for building further capacities in the country to meet its regional and international obligations. As an ASEAN member, Myanmar is no stranger to balancing regional interests with the need to acknowledge national (and local) sensitivities. Myanmar's interactions with EU may thus be informed by Myanmar's ASEAN experience.

In this essay, I examine how ASEAN's experience in dealing with Myanmar in reconciling regional and domestic interests can facilitate constructive outcomes for ASEAN-EU relations. There are three characteristics worth examining.

ASEAN Participation as a Dynamic Learning Process

Unlike Myanmar in 1997, which brought its sanctions baggage to ASEAN's discussions with the EU, Myanmar today can build on policy foundations and established working mechanisms for engaging with the EU as an ASEAN member. It is important to recall that ASEAN's position to the EU from the outset was to emphasise that Myanmar as an ASEAN member required equal treatment from ASEAN's dialogue partners.[1] That position, which ASEAN upholds towards its Dialogue Partners, continues to underscore ASEAN's preference to engage Myanmar in dialogue towards constructive outcomes (despite the frustrations attending such effort) rather than isolate it. This remains relevant in Myanmar's present political moment.

---

[1] ASEAN-EU meetings were postponed in the initial years after Myanmar's admission into ASEAN, over disagreements on the modality of Myanmar's participation (as an ASEAN member) at these meetings. The EU officials refused to sit at the same table with Myanmar officials, and did not wish to have the Myanmar flag displayed on the table. See Marchi, Ludovica (2014). Unmovable or Compromising? The European Union vis-à-vis Myanmar via EU-ASEAN: continuity and changes. The London School of Economics and Political Science, Centre for International Studies, London, UK, pp. 7–10 (http://eprints.lse.ac.uk/64794/). See also news releases on this topic compiled by the Transnational Institute, on "EU-ASEAN and the Case of Burma". (https://www.tni.org/en/article/eu-asean-and-the-case-of-burma)

Through ASEAN, Myanmar has learnt the importance of the links between national interests and regional commitments. The military regime had thought to use ASEAN membership as a shield. Instead, they faced the reality of having to report regularly to fellow ASEAN members on the human rights situation in Myanmar and the steps taken for democratisation and national reconciliation. In July 2005, the military regime bowed out of its rotational turn to chair ASEAN the following year, in recognition that its domestic situation presented more challenges than that of seeking external legitimacy through hosting and chairing ASEAN Summits. Several ASEAN Dialogue Partners, including the EU, had indicated to ASEAN their intention to downgrade their representation at ASEAN meetings under Myanmar's chairmanship, should that arise.

The 2008 Cyclone Nargis tragedy offered another lesson for Myanmar, and an opportunity to work for change through a humanitarian response coordinated by ASEAN. After the Union Solidarity and Development Party (USDP) government took office in 2011, President U Thein Sein, who had served as the military regime's Prime Minister in 2008, built on these lessons for the USDP's performance legitimacy. The USDP's policy framework for economic and social reforms in 2013 linked economic reform programmes to the ASEAN Economic Community (AEC) goals. In 2014, as the rotational ASEAN Chair for that year, Myanmar sought to uphold the regional (ASEAN) interest in negotiating consensus on an ASEAN position regarding territorial claims in the South China Sea. But in 2015, Myanmar was reluctant to engage with ASEAN member states over the Rohingya "boat people" crisis at sea. After the NLD government took office in 2016, however, ASEAN was the first multilateral forum Myanmar turned to regarding security issues in Rakhine State involving and affecting the Rohingya communities residing there. Daw Aung San Suu Kyi, in her capacity as Myanmar's Foreign Minister, briefed her counterparts at a special meeting in Yangon in November 2016. In the aftermath of the 2017 Rohingya exodus, Myanmar has again turned to ASEAN in dealing with the humanitarian and repatriation aspects of the issue.

Continued Engagement in Myanmar's Transition

The EU's interest to assist Myanmar's further integration into ASEAN underpins its in-country programmes in Myanmar.[2] There is some recognition that boosting economic performance may facilitate progress in the socio-political sphere. In August 2019, the EU committed to providing up to €8 million over four years to help Myanmar "integrate better with ASEAN economies in line with the ASEAN Economic Community Blueprint 2025".[3] This adds to bilateral aid to Myanmar for 2014 to 2020,[4] allocated across four priority areas: rural development, education, governance and peace.[5]

The EU's assistance for Myanmar's transition started after the USDP government amended legislation to enable the NLD, especially then opposition leader Daw Aung San Suu Kyi, to re-enter the political process, ceding parliamentary seats via by-elections in 2012. The EU Council Conclusions on Myanmar/Burma in 2013 called for a comprehensive framework to support the country's reform process, political, social and economic development, respect for human rights, and assisting the

---

[2] Dosch, Jörn, and Jatswan S. Sidhu (2015), The European Union's Myanmar Policy: Focused or Directionless?, in: Journal of Current Southeast Asian Affairs, 34, 2, 85–112. (https://journals.sub.uni-hamburg.de/giga/jsaa/article/viewFile/874/874-910-1-PB.pdf)

[3] Thiha Ko Ko, "€8 million funding for trade initiatives", Myanmar Times online edition, 12 August 2019. (https://www.mmtimes.com/news/eu8-million-funding-trade-initiatives.html)

[4] The EU's Multiannual Indicative Programme 2014-2020 for Myanmar had an indicative allocation of €688 million. The amount is listed as €656 million on the French Foreign Minsitry's website section on Myanmar, which includes a section on Myanmar's relations with the EU. See: https://www.diplomatie.gouv.fr/en/country-files/myanmar/

[5] Myanmar's relations with the European Union as listed on the French Foreign Ministry's website. (https://www.diplomatie.gouv.fr/en/country-files/myanmar/)

Myanmar government rebuild its international image.[6] Although the EU made its move in lockstep with the United States' stance to 'match action for action'[7], the EU was the first to lift sanctions in 2013. The same year the EU's Myanmar office (established in 2012) was elevated to full EU Delegation status. An EU-Myanmar Task Force, established in November 2013, coordinates the implementation of the EU's political and economic assistance.[8] In 2018, Myanmar was the second largest recipient of EU development assistance in Asia.[9]

Compared to the EU's reluctance to engage Myanmar under a military government as an equal participant in the ASEAN-EU dialogue, and its relatively low level of representation in Myanmar till 2013, the consultative dialogue and joint programming of development cooperation today is unprecedented in EU-Myanmar interactions. While the Rohingya issue has crystallised the urgency of re-establishing trust broken over decades among the different communities in Myanmar, it has also highlighted the long-term nature of this challenge. The priority areas of rural development, education, governance and peace are important pathways for building capacities to address egregious gaps in human rights in the country.

Creative Ways of a Collective Approach

Prior to 1996, the EU countries pursued individual policies in their interactions with Myanmar. This changed with the adoption of the EU's "Common Position on Burma" in 1996. With

---

[6] Council Conclusions on the Comprehensive Framework for the EU's Policy and Support to Myanmar/Burma, July 2013. (https://www.consilium.europa.eu/uedocs/cms_data/docs/pressdata/EN/foraff/138272.pdf)

[7] Enunciated by then US Secretary of State Hillary Clinton, in providing a cautious welcome to the reforms instituted by the USDP government.

[8] https://ec.europa.eu/commission/presscorner/detail/en/IP_13_1062

[9] Myanmar received 20% of funds allocated under the EU's Multiannual Indicative Programme for Asia. India and Vietnam received 14% each. (https://ec.europa.eu/international-partnerships/where-we-work/asia_en)

democracy and human rights being the cornerstones of the foreign policies of individual EU members, these principles became important components of the EU's collective position on Myanmar. At the 'height' of this policy, almost all forms of financial and technical assistance to Myanmar came to a standstill, including visa restrictions on the generals and members of the military regime, and revoking trade privileges accorded under the EU's Generalised Scheme of Preferences (GSP).[10] But individual EU members still nuanced their foreign (economic) policies towards Myanmar. France did not compel Total Oil to stop its operations in Myanmar. The United Kingdom — though driving policy pronouncements on Myanmar — was the top investor in Myanmar in 1997.[11] Despite the collective policy that advocated 'critical dialogue' over ASEAN's 'constructive engagement', some EU members were also "chafing at the hard line being pursued and seeking more pragmatic approaches".[12]

Myanmar reacted by seeking 'friends' elsewhere. As the ASEAN member states continued their bilateral relations with Myanmar after the military coup, Myanmar's top diplomats turned their attention to ASEAN membership.[13] For the technocrats, this move was to provide some space for manoeuvre

---

[10] Renaud Egreteau and Larry Jagan, *Soldiers and Diplomacy in Burma*, NUS Press, 2013, p. 212.

[11] A study carried out by a group of Myanmar economists under the auspices of the Center for Business Research and Development (CBRD), Faculty of Business Administration, National University of Singapore, stated that in 1997, UK emerged as the top investor ($1,305 billion), followed by Singapore ($1,215 billion), Thailand ($1,027 billion), France ($470.4 million), US ($582 million), Malaysia ($447.4 million), Indonesia ($208.95 million) and Japan ($192 million). See: Khin Maung Kyi, Ronald Findlay, R.M. Sundrum, Mya Maung, Myo Nyunt, Zaw Oo, et al. (2000). *A Vision and A Strategy: Economic Development of Burma*, Olof Palme International Center, Stockholm, Sweden, p. 110.

[12] Rodolfo Severino (2006). *Southeast Asia in Search of an ASEAN Community*. ISEAS: Singapore, 2006, pp. 330–331, 335–336.

[13] Personal interview with U Ohn Gyaw, Myanmar Foreign Minister from 1991 to 1998. He was the prime mover in persuading the junta to agree to Myanmar's ASEAN membership application.

amidst the restrictions imposed by the West.[14] However, the generals apparently viewed ASEAN membership as a step towards "gaining legitimacy at home and abroad".[15] Economically, ASEAN membership was also important, as Myanmar under the military regime faced sanctions and restrictions from the West. Myanmar viewed being part of ASEAN as having "greater cooperation with friends in the region" which would not require the country to "place more emphasis on investments from other parts of the world (Western hemisphere)".[16]

The EU position on political-security issues in Southeast Asia were not just on Myanmar. The EU had earlier raised with ASEAN the situation of the Indochinese asylum-seekers and the Cambodian question, including Vietnam's incursion into Cambodia, prior to their ASEAN membership. However, Myanmar has been most on the EU's discussion agenda with ASEAN before and after membership. Yet, the EU's interest to work with (and through) ASEAN on humanitarian assistance for Cyclone Nargis survivors can be interpreted as a turning point for EU policy. The Nargis tragedy led to a re-consideration of the EU's human security interpretation, broadening it to include the aftermath of natural disasters. This contextualisation was made possible through Myanmar's status as an ASEAN member, and the ASEAN-led response in Myanmar provided additional credibility.

From Critical Dialogue to Enhanced Engagement

Today, ASEAN's credibility is once again being tested by how Myanmar deals with the Rohingya repatriation. The 2020 State

---

[14] Ibid.

[15] Tin Maung Maung Than and Mya Than, "ASEAN Enlargement and Myanmar", Mya Than and Carolyn L. Gale (eds.), *ASEAN Enlargement: Impact and Implications*, ISEAS: Singapore, 2001, p. 252.

[16] Khin Ohn Thant, citing the New Light of Myanmar, in "ASEAN Enlargement: Economic and Financial Implications for Myanmar", Mya Than and Carolyn L. Gale (eds.), *ASEAN Enlargement: Impact and Implications*, ISEAS: Singapore, 2001, p. 264.

of Southeast Asia survey among policy elites in ASEAN member states sought views on "what should ASEAN do better to mitigate the Rakhine crisis". About 55% of the respondents were dissatisfied with ASEAN's handling of the issue. Of these respondents, 43% wished to see ASEAN mediating between the Myanmar government and the Rakhine and Rohingya communities. Apart from the Philippines and Indonesia, respondents from other ASEAN member states (including Myanmar) are reluctant to resettle the Rohingya in their country.[17]

This divisive issue — regionally and domestically — will be at the forefront of policy considerations and discussions, even as the EU seeks to implement a policy of enhanced engagement with Myanmar. A recently released report by the EU on this policy towards Bangladesh, Cambodia and Myanmar stated the EU's concerns on the non-implementation of human rights and labour conventions listed in the GSP Regulation, but that Myanmar had shown a "constructive attitude and engagement on the issues of concern raised by the EU". Some of these concerns included: combating hate speech, humanitarian access and conditions for internally displaced persons, implementing the recommendations of the Report of the Advisory Commission on Rakhine State, and ensuring accountability for human rights violations.[18]

The EU's enhanced engagement policy overlaps with ASEAN's interest in assisting Myanmar overcome these challenges. But ASEAN's approach is to nuance its collective response via bilateral projects or programmes. Adopting a

---

[17] Tang Siew Mun et al., *The State of Southeast Asia 2020 Survey Report*. Singapore: ISEAS-Yusof Ishak Institute, 2020. (https://www.iseas.edu.sg/images/pdf/TheStateofSEASurveyReport_2020.pdf)

[18] European Commission, High Representative of the Union of Foreign Affairs and Security Policy, "Report on EU Enhanced Engagement with three Everything But Arms beneficiary countries: Bangladesh, Cambodia and Myanmar", Brussels, 10 February 2020. (https://ec.europa.eu/transparency/regdoc/rep/10102/2020/EN/SWD-2020-19-F1-EN-MAIN-PART-1.PDF)

similar approach may help the EU give effect to its 'responsibility to protect' commitment, with an added 'responsibility to help'.[19] This may give the EU's Myanmar strategy the necessary traction to engage the NLD government in well-coordinated and cohesive programmes that complement bilateral programmes of EU members. The EU's long-standing relations with ASEAN can thus be brought to bear in helping Myanmar build capacities for active (and responsible) participation in regional integration.

---

[19] Moe Thuzar. "The EU and Myanmar in the post-2016 scenario", *The European Union and Myanmar: Interactions Via ASEAN*, Ludovica Marchi Balosi Restelli (ed.), Routledge, 2020.

14

Navigating the Nadir of Philippines-European Union Relations

Sol Iglesias

Since the election of President Rodrigo Duterte, the shift in the Southeast Asian nation's posture toward human rights and democracy has sent relations between the Philippines and the European Union (EU) to their lowest point. Thousands have been killed in the president's signature "war on drugs". The scale of violence and official impunity is unprecedented. Moreover, unlike any Filipino leader before him, Duterte explicitly rejects and attacks basic notions of democracy. This gives erstwhile allies, European states among them, very little purchase on which to exhort commonly held values. Still, a closer look at how relations have evolved in the early years of the Duterte presidency reveals that the Philippines has not been entirely hostile to cooperation. If it wants to be effective, the EU must be consistent and focused in its diplomacy. This essay provides an analysis of the tumultuous relations between the EU and the Philippines under Duterte, with recommendations for a way forward.

Overture

"I have read the condemnation of the European Union. I'm telling them, 'F**k you'", President Duterte stated on 21st September

2016, about a week after the European Parliament issued a resolution on the Philippines condemning the brutal anti-narcotic crackdown and extrajudicial killings. Later in that speech to local businessmen in his hometown of Davao City, he repeated the expletive and raised his middle finger as punctuation.[1]

The contrast with Duterte's predecessor, Benigno Aquino, could not be starker. During the Aquino administration, a Philippine-EU Partnership Cooperation Agreement (PCA) was signed in 2012.[2] In 2014, the Philippines successfully applied for a Special Incentive Arrangement for Sustainable Development and Good Governance under the EU's Generalised Scheme of Preferences (GSP+). GSP+ status offers preferential access to the EU market, aimed at developing countries unable to fully utilize existing favoured access to Europe and that furthermore lack export diversification and integration into global trade.[3] EU grant assistance for the Philippines for the period 2014 to 2020 doubled compared with the previous period (2007 to 2013) from 130 to 260 million euros, making the EU and its member states among the largest donors to the country.[4]

Why did relations between the Philippines and the EU deteriorate so badly?

The main source of tension is Duterte's anti-drug crime campaign and extrajudicial killings. From the day that Duterte took office in 2016 until 2019, local rights groups estimate that more than 27,000 have been killed in the president's anti-drug campaign while the Philippine National Police puts the number

---

[1] Ted Regencia, "Philippines' Duterte Unleashes More Profanity at the EU," *Al Jazeera*, September 21, 2016, https://www.aljazeera.com/news/2016/09/philippines-duterte-unleashes-profanity-eu-160920193250592.html.

[2] The agreement was delayed due to a case brought by the European Commission to the European Court of Justice and entered into force only in 2018.

[3] Currently, the Philippines is one of only eight countries with GSP+ status. "Mid-Term Evaluation of the EU Generalised Scheme of Preferences: Final Interim Report," (Brussels: European Commission, 2017), 26-30.

[4] European External Action Service, "Philippines and the EU," https://eeas.europa.eu/delegations/philippines/1694/philippines-and-eu_en.

at 5,552.[5] The United Nations Human Rights Council (HRC), in a 2019 resolution, called on the Philippine government to take all necessary measures to prevent extrajudicial killings and forced disappearances. The HRC mandated the High Commissioner to report at the Council's 44th session in 2020.[6]

This violence is unprecedented. Even under the notoriously violent Marcos dictatorship, there were an estimated 2,427 extrajudicial killings from 1975 to 1985.[7]

On the whole, the regime's lurch towards authoritarianism is unmistakable. On the 25th of May, 2017, Duterte imposed martial law in Mindanao, the southernmost of the country's three main island groups, in response to a terrorist attack there in Marawi City. Upon lifting military rule in Mindanao on 31st December 2019, the government clarified that the whole country remains in a state of national emergency by virtue of a proclamation issued on the 4th of September, 2016. In the post-Marcos, democratic period, such measures hitherto have been very rarely used and limited to short periods of time as well as to specific provinces only. Duterte is the first Philippine president to not render "even the minimum obeisance to liberal democratic politics" nor to emulate the policy affirmations of democratic values espoused by post-Marcos presidents.[8]

Indeed, the European Parliament asked the EU Delegation to the Philippines to carefully monitor this use of emergency powers. The Parliament's 2016 resolution objected to President

---

[5] Human Rights Watch, "Philippines: No Letup in 'Drug War' Killings," January 14, 2020, https://www.hrw.org/news/2020/01/14/philippines-no-letup-drug-war-killings.

[6] United Nations Human Rights Council, "41st Session of the Human Rights Council: Resolution on the Promotion and Protection of Human Rights in the Philippines Adopted 11 July 2019."

[7] Estimate of extrajudicial killings from 1975 to 1985. Richard Kessler, *Rebellion and Repression in the Philippines* (New Haven: Yale University Press, 1989), 137.

[8] Lisandro Claudio and Patricio Abinales, "Dutertismo, Maoismo, Nasyonalismo," in *A Duterte Reader: Critical Essays on Rodrigo Duterte's Early Presidency*, ed. Nicole Curato (Ithaca: Cornell University Press, 2017), 93–94.

Duterte's statements urging law enforcement agencies and the public to kill suspected drug traffickers. Parliament thus called upon the EU to use "all available instruments to assist the Government of the Philippines in respecting its international human rights obligations".[9] It was this resolution that sparked the president's ire, signalling a new and antagonistic attitude towards the EU.

Escalation

The current discord between the Philippines and the EU is rooted in a fundamental conflict between the concept of non-interference in the Association of Southeast Asian Nations (ASEAN) and the EU's use of political conditionality in its external relations, linked to trade and economic ties particularly.

ASEAN, originally an anti-communist bloc, bases its cooperation on protecting each member from external interference in domestic affairs. The Treaty of Amity and Cooperation in Southeast Asia, signed at the first ASEAN summit on the 24th of February 1976 refers to "the right of every State to lead its national existence free from external interference, subversion or coercion" as well as "non-interference in the internal affairs of one another".[10] Non-interference is invoked to reject inconvenient foreign pressure. Following the end of the Cold War, reformers within ASEAN emerged to espouse "constructive engagement", in which the manifest interest of ASEAN states in their fellow members could be expressed and actions taken without requiring consensus.[11] Nevertheless, the "ASEAN Way" of non-interference prevails as the overriding principle. In the Philippines, the government of the day has made it amply clear that it will not tolerate criticism.

---

[9] "European Parliament Resolution of 15 September 2016 on the Philippines."
[10] "Treaty of Amity and Cooperation in Southeast Asia, Indonesia, 24 February 1976," https://asean.org/treaty-amity-cooperation-southeast-asia-indonesia-24-february-1976/.
[11] Yu Ping Chan, "Standing By: ASEAN in Crisis," *Harvard International Review* 23, no. 1 (2001).

In the context of the EU, political conditionality refers to the linking of certain values or norms such as human rights protection and the advancement of democratic principles to benefits such as trade and aid.[12] Conditionalities have been integrated into trade relations, treaties and general relations with external parties. Consequently, the EU is often characterized as a normative power, particularly in universalizing human rights standards and social norms.[13]

In this regard, the GSP is one of the main instruments that the EU uses to link social and human rights issues to trade. GSP+ status requires that the beneficiaries have ratified 27 conventions, including human rights treaties, and subjects them to monitoring in order to determine if serious and systematic violations of labour and human rights have occurred. The European Commission (EC) can temporarily withdraw GSP+ privileges from all or certain products as a consequence.

The European Parliament issued a 2017 resolution condemning the high number of extrajudicial killings related to the anti-drug campaign. The European Parliament viewed the summary killings, as well as other matters like the reinstatement of the death penalty and lowering the minimum age for criminal responsibility, as violations by the Philippines of treaty obligations. Thus, the resolution asked the EC to use all means to persuade the Philippines to put an end to the violence including "procedural steps with a view to the possible removal of GSP+ preferences".[14]

The parliamentary resolution also sought for the immediate release of Senator Leila de Lima, who had been arrested and

---

[12] Karen Smith, "The Use of Political Conditionality in the European Union's Relations with Third Countries: How Effective?," *European Foreign Affairs Review* (1998).

[13] Clair Gammage, "A Critique of the Extraterritorial Obligations of the EU in Relation to Human Rights Clauses and Social Norms in EU Free Trade Agreements," *Europe and the World: A law review* 2, no. 1 (2018): 2–3.

[14] "European Parliament Resolution of 16 March 2017 on the Philippines — the Case of Senator Leila M. De Lima."

detained on charges that she accepted money from drug dealers while Secretary of Justice of the previous administration. De Lima is a top critic of President Duterte, whom she had investigated both in the Senate and the Commission on Human Rights. It is of no small significance that the resolution highlighted de Lima's case in its title.

The European Parliament sought to invoke political conditionalities tied to preferential trade arrangements in a move that the Philippine government considered as meddling in its domestic affairs.

Rapprochement?

In light of the possibility that the EU would yank away trade privileges from the Philippines, the action shifted in arena from President Duterte's immediate ambit to that of technocracy and diplomacy.

On the 4th of July 2017 in Manila, the European External Action Service (EEAS) and the Philippine Department of Foreign Affairs held a ninth senior officials' meeting, which had been last held as far back as 2013. Talks included the GSP+ as well as a "candid exchange of views on the human rights situation in the Philippines and the EU".[15] The GSP+ status of the Philippines was under review at the time, with a second biennial report due in early 2018.

Subsequently, the secretary of the Department of Trade and Industry, Ramon Lopez, and the late Edgardo Angara, who had been appointed special envoy to the EU, were dispatched to Brussels. They made a presentation to the European Parliament and conducted several meetings with EU officials "to ensure continuity of the GSP+ privilege".[16] Other signs of rapprochement

---

[15] "Joint Press Statement on the 9th PH-EU Senior Officials' Meeting," 4 July 2017.
[16] A.G.A. Mogato, "PHL Moves to Assure EU on GSP+ Fitness," *Business World*, September 28, 2017.

included the appointment of a Philippine ambassador to the EU after a long vacancy and an unprecedented invitation to European Council president Donald Tusk as a guest of the Chair at the 12th East Asia Summit in Manila.[17]

Finally, in January 2018, the EU concluded the review process and affirmed that the Philippines would retain its GSP+ status. The biennial report (2016 to 2017) of the EC and the European Council noted that the Philippines had increased its use of GSP+ preferences to 26% of its total exports, with a GSP+ utilisation rate of 71% in 2016. Moreover, Philippine exports grew 51% since 2012, due in great part to this enhanced access to the EU market.[18]

On the other hand, the report carried the concerns of the European Parliament over the "war on drugs", systematic rights violations, as well as incitement to violence and impunity. These issues will be significant in future reviews, particularly in light of the EC's partial withdrawal of tariff preferences to Cambodia under the EU's Everything-But-Arms (EBA) trade scheme on 12th February 2020 over human rights violations and warnings that Myanmar may similarly lose its EBA privileges.[19]

Another source of friction between the Philippines and the EU had been over the question of development aid. The Duterte administration rejected 250 million euros in new EU grants, 39 million euros in sustainable energy projects and 6.1 million euros

---

[17] Paterno Esmaquel II, "Behind the Scenes, PH Scrambles to Mend EU Ties," *Rappler*, December 7, 2017, https://www.rappler.com/nation/190664-philippines-european-union-eu-relations-duterte.

[18] "The EU Special Incentive Arrangement for Sustainable Development and Good Governance ('GSP+') Assessment of the Philippines Covering the Period 2016–2017," (Brussels: European Commission, High Representative of the Union for Foreign Affairs and Security Policy, 2018).

[19] European Commission, "Trade/Human Rights: Commission Decides to Partially Withdraw Cambodia's Preferential Access to the EU Market," 12 February 2020, https://ec.europa.eu/commission/presscorner/detail/en/ip_20_229. See also "Myanmar: EU Mission Assesses Human Rights and Labour Rights Situation," 31 October 2018, http://trade.ec.europa.eu/doclib/press/index.cfm?id=1936.

worth of trade-related technical assistance, refusing the imposition of conditionalities relating to human rights and the "war on drugs".[20] However, matters seemed to right themselves when the 2012 PCA framework agreement finally entered into force on the 1st of March 2018. A few days later, the EC clarified that aid relations would proceed as normal without any rejections from the Philippine side, contradicting earlier pronouncements on the matter.[21]

Yet the situation quickly changed once more. Another European Parliament resolution on the Philippines was made on the 19th of April 2018 recognising that the ratification of the PCA affirmed the joint commitment of the Philippines and the EU to, *inter alia*, good governance, democracy, the rule of law and human rights.[22] Building upon the previous parliamentary resolutions, the statement furthermore welcomed the International Criminal Court investigation of crimes against humanity in the Philippines and advocated to remove the Philippines from the HRC before its term expired. In other statements, the EU also welcomed the HRC's decision to investigate the Philippines as well as expressed concern over the removal of Chief Justice Maria Lourdes Sereno and judicial independence.[23]

Free Trade Agreement (FTA) negotiations that the Philippines and the EU had contemplated in 2016 have been in limbo since

---

[20] Paterno Esmaquel II, "Philippines Formally Rejects P380 Million in EU Aid," *Rappler*, January 24, 2018, https://www.rappler.com/nation/194426-philippines-formally-rejects-european-union-aid.

[21] Jenny Lei Ravelo, "After a Tumultuous Year, EU Aid to Continue in the Philippines," *Devex*, March 5, 2018, https://www.devex.com/news/after-a-tumultuous-year-eu-aid-to-continue-in-the-philippines-92247.

[22] "European Parliament Resolution of 19 April 2018 on the Philippines."

[23] European External Action Service, "EU Annual Report on Human Rights and Democracy in the World 2018: Philippines Country Update," (Brussels: EEAS, 2019).

July 2019.[24] This was a blow to the Philippine aim of expanding access to the European market beyond GSP+ and with the greater stability that a FTA could offer. While it is in Europe's strategic interest to construct its trading architecture with Japan and ASEAN markets, the violence and European Parliament resolutions compelled the EU to re-evaluate the necessity of an FTA with the Philippines.[25]

A Hard Road Ahead

The Philippines and the EU relationship has never been more fraught with complications. Nonetheless, this analysis has demonstrated that the Philippines has not been entirely hostile to the EU's response to the grave human rights situation in the Philippines. Progress can be made if the Philippines continues to reaffirm respect for the rule of law and the human rights of its citizens. The relationship between the EU and the Philippines will only worsen unless the Duterte government provides guarantees that the level of violence will not escalate further.

On the other hand, the EU needs to recognise the limits of its influence as the Philippines actively diversifies its economic, diplomatic and security relations with other stakeholders—most notably China.[26] Underpinning Duterte's bellicose behaviour is the confidence that stems from an economy that

---

[24] Roy Stephen Canivel, "Human Rights Concerns Stall PH Free Trade Talks with EU," *Philippine Daily Inquirer*, July 8, 2019, https://business.inquirer.net/274157/human-rights-concerns-stall-ph-free-trade-talks-with-eu. See also Bernie Cahiles-Magkilat, "EU Not Keen on FTA Talks with PH," *Manila Bulletin*, January 27, 2020, https://business.mb.com.ph/2020/01/26/eu-not-keen-on-fta-talks-with-ph/.

[25] Hanna Deringer and Hosuk Lee-Makiyama, "Europe and South-East Asia: An Exercise in Diplomatic Patience," in *ECIPE Policy Brief, No. 5/2018* (Brussels: European Centre for International Political Economy (ECIPE), 2018), 10–12.

[26] Olli Suorsa and Mark Thompson, "Choosing Sides? Illiberalism and Hedging in the Philippines and Thailand," *Panorama*, no. 2 (2017).

grew annually at 6.3% on average from 2010 to 2018 with declining poverty, inequality and unemployment rates.[27]

To move forward, the Philippine government must also allow for independent investigations to begin. Regardless of President Duterte's public statements against allowing access to United Nations Special Rapporteur on Extrajudicial Killings, for instance, it is important to acknowledge that such a measure is not without precedent. In 2007, President Gloria Macapagal Arroyo acquiesced to exactly this kind of inquiry over allegations of state-sponsored violence against leftist activists and other violations.[28] The president's earlier statements that uniformed personnel and members of the public would not be prosecuted for the killings are untenable and need to be withdrawn. Local investigations and prosecutions into specific cases must begin as a sign that this violent chapter is at an end.

Likewise, the EU has shown a willingness to find ways to cooperate with the Philippines while maintaining that respect for human rights is indispensable. The EU has been inconsistent and lacked focus, however. This blunts the full positive effect of what it can achieve with the Philippine government. Instead, it should concentrate its diplomatic efforts on ending on-going violence and preventing any new escalation.

To do so, the EU must demonstrate that it is responsive to on-going developments inside the Philippines rather than in Brussels. Thus far, engagement and disengagement reflected very little of the actual human rights situation in the country. Efforts to document human rights violations and track the number of cases need support. Using such empirical evidence, the EU should

---

[27] Poverty declined from 26.6 % in 2006 to 21.6 % in 2015 while the Gini coefficient declined from 42.9 to 40.1 over the same period. Unemployment has reached historic low rates. The World Bank, "The World Bank in the Philippines: Overview," November 25, 2019, https://www.worldbank.org/en/country/philippines/overview.

[28] See Peter Sales, "State Terror in the Philippines: The Alston Report, Human Rights and Counter-Insurgency under the Arroyo Administration," *Contemporary Politics* 15, no. 3 (2009).

respond to escalations in violence using instruments available to them as well as encourage cessation and decline in violence.

The European Parliament has played an extremely important role in Philippine-EU relations under Duterte by applying pressure on the other EU institutions and demonstrating an unrelenting line on respect for human rights. However, the Parliament has failed to issue any resolution on the Philippines since 2018. The Parliament needs to continue to monitor the situation and provide the EC and the EEAS political direction vis-à-vis the Philippines. Future resolutions need to narrow their focus on some achievable goals such as on GSP+ monitoring, freeing Senator de Lima and other political detainees, tracking the levels of violence in a verifiable manner, and securing the unconditional visit of the relevant UN special rapporteurs.

If both sides are able to learn from the twists and turns of the last few years, it may be possible for the Philippines and the EU to navigate a way out of these depths.

References

Cahiles-Magkilat, Bernie. "EU Not Keen on FTA Talks with PH." *Manila Bulletin*. Published electronically January 27, 2020. https://business.mb.com.ph/2020/01/26/eu-not-keen-on-fta-talks-with-ph/.

Canivel, Roy Stephen. "Human Rights Concerns Stall PH Free Trade Talks with EU." *Philippine Daily Inquirer*. Published electronically July 8, 2019. https://business.inquirer.net/274157/human-rights-concerns-stall-ph-free-trade-talks-with-eu.

Chan, Yu Ping. "Standing By: ASEAN in Crisis." *Harvard International Review* 23, no. 1 (2001).

Claudio, Lisandro, and Patricio Abinales. "Dutertismo, Maoismo, Nasyonalismo." In *A Duterte Reader: Critical Essays on Rodrigo Duterte's Early Presidency*, edited by Nicole Curato, 167–98. Ithaca: Cornell University Press, 2017.

Deringer, Hanna, and Hosuk Lee-Makiyama. "Europe and South-East Asia: An Exercise in Diplomatic Patience." In *ECIPE Policy Brief, No. 5/2018*. Brussels: European Centre for International Political Economy (ECIPE), 2018.

Esmaquel II, Paterno. "Behind the Scenes, PH Scrambles to Mend EU Ties." *Rappler*. Published electronically December 7, 2017. https://www.rappler.com/nation/190664-philippines-european-union-eu-relations-duterte.

———. "Philippines Formally Rejects P380 Million in EU Aid." *Rappler*. Published electronically January 24, 2018. https://www.rappler.com/nation/194426-philippines-formally-rejects-european-union-aid.

"The EU Special Incentive Arrangement for Sustainable Development and Good Governance ('GSP+') Assessment of the Philippines Covering the Period 2016–2017." Brussels:

European Commission, High Representative of the Union for Foreign Affairs and Security Policy, 2018.

European Commission. "Myanmar: EU Mission Assesses Human Rights and Labour Rights Situation." Published electronically 31 October 2018. http://trade.ec.europa.eu/doclib/press/index.cfm?id=1936.

———. "Trade/Human Rights: Commission Decides to Partially Withdraw Cambodia's Preferential Access to the EU Market." Published electronically 12 February 2020. https://ec.europa.eu/commission/presscorner/detail/en/ip_20_229.

European External Action Service. "EU Annual Report on Human Rights and Democracy in the World 2018: Philippines Country Update." Brussels: EEAS, 2019.

———. "Philippines and the EU." https://eeas.europa.eu/delegations/philippines/1694/philippines-and-eu_en.

"European Parliament Resolution of 15 September 2016 on the Philippines."

"European Parliament Resolution of 16 March 2017 on the Philippines — the Case of Senator Leila M. De Lima."

"European Parliament Resolution of 19 April 2018 on the Philippines."

Gammage, Clair. "A Critique of the Extraterritorial Obligations of the EU in Relation to Human Rights Clauses and Social Norms in EU Free Trade Agreements." *Europe and the World: A law review* 2, no. 1 (2018): 1–20.

Human Rights Watch. "Philippines: No Letup in 'Drug War' Killings." Published electronically January 14, 2020. https://www.hrw.org/news/2020/01/14/philippines-no-letup-drug-war-killings.

"Joint Press Statement on the 9th PH-EU Senior Officials' Meeting." Published electronically 4 July 2017.

Kessler, Richard. *Rebellion and Repression in the Philippines.* New Haven: Yale University Press, 1989.

"Mid-Term Evaluation of the EU Generalised Scheme of Preferences: Final Interim Report." Brussels: European Commission, 2017.

Mogato, A.G.A. "PHL Moves to Assure EU on GSP+ Fitness." *Business World.* Published electronically September 28, 2017.

Ravelo, Jenny Lei. "After a Tumultuous Year, EU Aid to Continue in the Philippines." *Devex.* Published electronically March 5, 2018. https://www.devex.com/news/after-a-tumultuous-year-eu-aid-to-continue-in-the-philippines-92247.

Regencia, Ted. "Philippines' Duterte Unleashes More Profanity at the EU." *Al Jazeera.* Published electronically September 21, 2016. https://www.aljazeera.com/news/2016/09/philippines-duterte-unleashes-profanity-eu-160920193250592.html.

Sales, Peter. "State Terror in the Philippines: The Alston Report, Human Rights and Counter-Insurgency under the Arroyo Administration." *Contemporary Politics* 15, no. 3 (2009): 321–36.

Smith, Karen. "The Use of Political Conditionality in the European Union's Relations with Third Countries: How Effective?". *European Foreign Affairs Review* (1998).

Suorsa, Olli, and Mark Thompson. "Choosing Sides? Illiberalism and Hedging in the Philippines and Thailand." *Panorama*, no. 2 (2017): 63–76.

The World Bank. "The World Bank in the Philippines: Overview." Published electronically November 25, 2019. https://www.worldbank.org/en/country/philippines/overview.

"Treaty of Amity and Cooperation in Southeast Asia, Indonesia, 24 February 1976." https://asean.org/treaty-amity-cooperation-southeast-asia-indonesia-24-february-1976/.

United Nations Human Rights Council. "41st Session of the Human Rights Council: Resolution on the Promotion and Protection of Human Rights in the Philippines Adopted 11 July 2019."

15

The Perception-Expectations Gap
Recalibrating Singapore-EU Relations

Yeo Lay Hwee

When examining Singapore relations with the European Union (EU), it is perhaps better to situate it in the broader context of Singapore's relations with Europe and the inter-regional dialogue between the EU and the Association of Southeast Asian Nations (ASEAN).

The Singapore Ministry of Foreign Affairs website does not have a section or official write-up on Singapore's relations with the EU. Instead, this important relationship is subsumed under the broader ambit of Singapore's relations with Europe, which includes countries in Europe from the far north such as Iceland to the West (Germany, France, etc) and from Central and Eastern Europe to the Caucasus and the Black Sea regions.

The EU is a longstanding partner of ASEAN — formal relations with ASEAN was established in 1977 with the European Economic Community (EEC), the predecessor of the EU. Singapore is a founding member of ASEAN and has played, and continues to play an active part in the development of ASEAN. Hence, EU-Singapore relations must also be viewed through the lens of the trials and tribulations in the development of EU-ASEAN partnership. It has not been always smooth sailing as Chapter One of the essay sets out. But the partnership has certainly been enriched and strengthened over the last decade.

The European External Action Service (EEAS) website proclaimed that the EU views Singapore as central to its engagement with Southeast Asia, and that Singapore is a key partner in a dynamic and rapidly evolving region. Thus, it was perhaps not surprising that Singapore is the first Southeast Asian country to conclude a Free Trade Agreement (FTA) with the EU.

Merchandise trade between the EU and Singapore and trade in services accounted for almost 24% and 58% respectively of EU-ASEAN trade. Singapore is the EU's largest investment destination in Asia. More than 10,000 EU companies are based in Singapore, using it as a hub for their operations in Southeast Asia. Conversely, Singapore is the EU's third largest Asian investor after Japan and Hong Kong.

These trade and investment figures has the potential for further growth now that the EU-Singapore Free Trade Agreement (EUSFTA) has come into effect.

So why is it that despite such "glowing figures" the EU is relatively unknown in Singapore?

Perceptions and Expectations:

There are several reasons. First, when people look at trade and investments, they see French wine, German cars, Italian pasta, Spanish olive oil; additionally, Singaporeans may work for companies like Siemens, BNP Paribas, IKEA, etc., which they see through national lens — Siemens is a German company, BNP a French international bank, and IKEA Swedish. Diplomatic relations is also viewed primarily through a national lens. The very strong bilateral ties that Singapore enjoys with many EU member states sometimes obscure the importance of the EU.

Secondly, there is also general confusion of Europe as a geographical term and Europe as a political entity. European politicians from the EU member states often loosely use Europe (a geographical construct) to refer to the EU (a political and economic entity) and the mass media is often as guilty. It is no wonder that many Singaporeans are not sure which countries are in the European Union and how is EU different from Europe.

Thirdly, the EU is indeed a complex political and economic entity that is difficult for ordinary people to fathom. The EU is a result of a very ambitious project of regional integration that began with the European Coal and Steel Community (ECSC) in the early 1950s to the European Economic Community in the sixties to the eighties. For European citizens where EU is a 'daily or lived reality' they have to grapple with what the EU is doing as EU policies and regulations have an impact — whether directly on their lives (such as the free mobile roaming which make their lives much better) or indirectly through how businesses are regulated and environment is protected. The informed ones will go a step to understand the national-regional nexus and try to understand the "Europeanisation" of their own societies. However, for those of us outside the EU, misconceptions of the EU are common.

In Singapore, this is not helped by the fact that the mass media here gets its news on Europe and the EU largely from English language news agencies such as Reuters, Associated Press, or op-eds or opinion pieces sourced from the UK (such as *Financial Times*) or from the US (such as *The New York Times*) which are perceived to be Eurosceptic. Our own mainstream media, *The Straits Times*, has been criticised for not having a correspondent in Brussels. Instead, reports and commentaries on the EU and European politics were filed from a correspondent based in London filtered through a Eurosceptic lens.

A much more problematic perception which is widespread not only among the public but also amongst some policy makers is the view that the EU is a less important political, security and economic actor than the US or China. This has shown up in perceptions survey in 2006 and 2011. The most recent survey done by the ISEAS-Yusof Ishak Institute (2020) on perceptions in Southeast Asia again reflected doubts about the EU's political and strategic influence. However, a positive aspect in the latest survey is that the EU comes out top as an organisation that can be trusted to uphold international law and the rules-based order. 36.5% of Singaporeans have confidence in the EU to provide leadership to maintain the rules-based order and uphold international law. The EU is also trusted to a good degree to champion global free trade, just behind Japan. These sentiments of course are expressed in the shadow of the intense rivalry between the US and China. In seeking out third parties to hedge against the uncertainties of the US-China rivalry, 41.9% of Singaporeans (highest amongst all ASEAN countries) singled out the EU.

Building on Trust and Momentum

If one is to take the latest survey result seriously, the time is right for the strengthening of not only the bilateral ties between the EU and Singapore, but for both to work together to enhance EU-ASEAN engagement, to hedge against the increasingly volatile and uncertain global environment.

First, bilaterally, Singapore and the EU can do much more to help business and companies translate the opportunities and potential of the EUSFTA into reality. This is especially important for Small and Medium Enterprises (SMEs). The business chambers and federation have an important role to play in raising awareness and providing informed advice about the EUSFTA, and helping Singapore SMEs to venture into Europe via the EU and for European SMEs to venture to Asia or ASEAN via Singapore.

Politically, the EU and Singapore, which benefitted from being open and embracing globalisation, and are firm supporters of multilateralism and a rule-based order, have to work far more closely across different platforms to support peace and stability. Besides the obvious EU-ASEAN platform, the EU and

Singapore can be partners across a number of issues utilizing and facilitating different channels to focus on the substance of the issues while being mindful of the possible obstacles and obstruction. In short, focus on what can be done and not pontificate over what should be done.

Take for example the US undermining of the WTO; the EU has pragmatically reached an agreement with 16 other WTO members, including China and Singapore, to establish an adhoc appeal body to overcome the US blockage of the global trade-dispute settlement system. In the midst of the Covid-19 pandemic, the US in its blame game and rivalry against China has accused the World Health Organisation (WHO) of being China-centric and threatened to withhold funding from it. The EU and its member states have in response, stepped up their pledge to continue support of the WHO.

Taking this approach, there is much that the EU and Singapore can work together not only to improve their bilateral ties, but become real partners in supporting regional and global cooperation. The urgency for more coordination and cooperation — through adhoc platforms of coalition of the willing or established channels such as the EU-ASEAN ministerial meeting or Asia-Europe Meeting (ASEM) is stark in the face of the greatest crisis facing all of us.

As the Covid-19 pandemic changes the nature and content of trade, digital trade and services would surely soar in importance. In these, there are still no global or even regional agreement as to the rules that should be applied. The digital economy, which is worth more than three trillion dollars, is now governed by a hodgepodge of rules, some of which exist in the WTO and others that are being developed in free trade agreements between different countries. The EU and Singapore which have been at the forefront of free trade agreements could take the lead in convening regional and inter-regional meetings on digital trade governance to develop a set of standards and guidelines (if not global rules) that can provide enough confidence and protection for the digital trade to continue to grow.

Another important area for dialogue and cooperation is in climate action and climate diplomacy. The EU has been in the forefront of climate diplomacy and climate action. The new Commission of the EU led by President Ursula von der Leyen has promised to face the climate challenge and take a holistic approach to examine all issues that can affect the climate agenda — from financial regulations to chemical rules, pollution standards for cars to the bloc's trading relationship with the rest of the world. The Commission's ambitious agenda on climate action has significant implications for its relations with third countries, and Singapore need to be actively engaged in dialogue with the EU on this because of the potential impact it might have on the EU's broader trade and economic relations with ASEAN. How can the EU's ambitious agenda on climate action be translated to supportive sustainability polices that can serve to strengthen its partnership with ASEAN rather than undermine it? These issues need critical reflections and pragmatic actions. Singapore can play an important role as coordinator for ASEAN's dialogue with the EU to explore pathways ahead and lay the foundations for a fruitful dialogue on sustainability policies.

Rising intolerance, racism and xenophobia, which were also amply displayed during the Covid-19 pandemic are also issues that both the EU and Singapore can work together to address. Immediately after the 911 terror attacks there was a realization that a global dialogue on Cultures and Civilisations is necessary to promote greater understanding and prevent Islamophobia. Yet, almost two decades later what we are witnessing is rising intolerance across nations fueled in part by the disinformation, fake news that are being transmitted through the social media. How to regulate the internet and social media platforms, how to address the challenges of echo chambers, fake news and disinformation, and how to promote religious and ethnic harmony — all these are issues that can benefit from greater societal exchange and policy dialogue without preconception of an ideal model or the superiority of any existing system.

Both the EU and Singapore face increasing pressures as the rivalry between China and America intensify. For the EU, America is its longtime ally but China is an increasingly important market, and the EU also recognized the fact that many of the global problems that we face such as climate change, and pandemics (as the Covid-19 virus outbreak manifest) cannot be solved without China's cooperation. For Singapore, China is a geographical reality in our region, and feels its weight much more than the EU. At the same time, Singapore also appreciates the strategic importance of the US in the region. Both are Singapore's key trading and investment partners. Navigating the tensions between the two and not having to choose sides is the ideal scenario for both Singapore and the EU. Yet, the US recent efforts to paint China as an enemy, its sharp rhetoric and now the blame game over Covid-19 risks a self-fulfilling prophecy of pushing the world into a new Cold War which portends accidental escalation to a real war. How can the EU, its member states and Singapore work to prevent such a scenario from becoming reality? We need to step up in various forums to provide that voice of reason and double down on our efforts to push back against unreasonable demands from either the US or China, and work towards pragmatic cooperation with both.

Conclusion

The EU and Singapore may appear on first glance to be two very different entities — a community of 27 nation-states versus a small city-state. Yet, the success of both the EU and Singapore are built upon reasonable politics and rational policies — one that has its beginning in the good luck of having visionary political leaders and committed technocrats. While both face immense challenges as we enter into an era fuel by the politics of fear and identity, and shortsighted policies driven by populism, they should remain steadfast to the fundamental values that have made them successful. They need to work closely in partnership with each other and with the member states of the EU and ASEAN to bring about peace and development in their respective regions.

16

Thailand-EU Ties
A Toxic Love Affair

Kavi Chongkittavorn

On the website of Thailand's Ministry of Foreign Affairs, it was proudly announced that on 21 February 2019, Thailand was ranked second in the 3rd Stop IUU Fishing Award, organised by the International Monitoring, Control and Surveillance Network, for the project entitled "Fish Product Traceability System: The Key Tool for Combating IUU Fishing of Thailand".

It was the project submitted by the Department of Fisheries, Ministry of Agriculture and Cooperatives, which for years, was blamed as the main culprit for illegal fishing in the kingdom. The award's announcement at the 6th Global Fisheries Enforcement Training Workshop in Bangkok was not featured in any media platform. The Thai public has not paid any attention to any good deed the military junta has done. The Thai media, politicians, trawler owners and fishing communities throughout the coastal provinces were unanimous in condemning the actions taken by the junta in complying with the EU's demands.

For the Thai authorities, involved in the three year-long struggle to combat the issue of illegal fishing from 2015 to January 2019, it was a testimony to their hard work and determination to correct the misconduct of Thailand's fishing industry. They did it under heavy pressure from the EU, which issued a yellow card pertaining to the country's bad records of over fishing, human rights violations, modern slavery practiced by the Thai fish trawlers. The EU repeatedly threatened the Thai military junta that it would not allow Thai marine products to enter the EU market, which is Thailand's biggest export market. In addition, the EU also halted all negotiations with Thailand over their bilateral free trade agreement.

Brussels' strong pressure worked for two reasons. First, it was the absolute power under the Article 44 of the Thai constitution, which empowered the military junta leader, Prime Minister General Prayut Chan-Ocha, to punish those who were previously unpunishable, both in the intra-government agencies and private sector. In previous governments, efforts were made but without any substantive results. Indeed, General Prayut singlehandedly altered the dynamic of Thai trawlers' overfishing in the Gulf of Thailand. Without the absolute power that the military government enjoyed then, numerous fisheries governance and good practices measures demanded by the EU could not have been enforced effectively, due to the bureaucratic bottle-necks and vested interests. New rules to vessel monitoring systems, a satellite-based system of tracking the movement of fishing boats, enforced by the Royal Thai Navy, are the signature outcome of the military junta.

Second, more than the EU would like to admit, Brussels threatened Thailand harshly for the May coup of 2014. The coup came as a surprise for the Western countries as they thought that Thai democracy had taken root. To them, Thailand's democratic development was steady and had been improving greatly since the 2006 coup. Worse of all, both the US and Europe thought the military establishments lied as they had promised that there would be no more power-seizure. Therefore, it was a huge sense of let-down in Brussels and its subsequent reactions revealed the European dismay as well as bias. As such, the yellow card against over-fishing and human rights violations was a ready-made tool kit that could be used to punish Thailand for staging a coup against a democratically elected government, headed by the country's first woman prime minister. That is the outcome of the toxic ties with the EU.

As the coordinating country for ASEAN-EU relations (2015-2018), Thailand has tried to push this problematic relationship to a new level. But Bangkok was unsuccessful as the EU bureaucrats continued their traditional and somewhat arrogant approach in criticizing the ASEAN members over their values and norms related to human rights and developmental approaches. Other ASEAN members described the EU approach as a case of double standards.

When Thailand chaired the ASEAN-EU foreign ministerial meeting in January 2019, Bangkok tried to push its ASEAN colleagues to officially announce European Union as a strategic partner. The time was ripe as other ASEAN dialogue partners, which were less significant, such as Russia, was upgraded as the grouping's eighth strategic partner.

The joint statement released after their meeting read: "We reaffirm the significant role played by ASEAN and the European Union in shaping the political, socio-economic and security agenda for both regions and globally, and agree in principle to upgrade EU-ASEAN relations to a Strategic Partnership, subject to details and timing to be worked out."

What was absent from the joint statement were the reasons which ASEAN used to delay the announcement of EU strategic partnership. After all, the EU has been the grouping's oldest dialogue partner with a long history of 44 years. Unfortunately, the length of their relationship has not been a good criterion to gauge the level of affinity between the two groupings. Indonesia and Malaysia opposed the move to declare the EU as the latest strategic partner unless the EU settled the issue related to palm oil. These two ASEAN members are the world's largest exporters. Currently, both sides have formed working groups to find common solutions. Furthermore, the domestic developments in Cambodia and Myanmar had attracted scrutiny and potentially punitive measures, from the EU.

EU prejudice aside, ASEAN really needs the EU to counterbalance the strategic influence of US and China. After President Donald Trump took power in 2017, shifts of US attitude and policies toward the EU over security and trade prompted Brussels to further strengthen non-economic ties, especially in strategic matters. Thailand was able to persuade the Philippine chair in 2017 to invite the President of the European Council, Donald Tusk, to take part in a pre-East Asia Summit meeting with other world leaders. Since 2017, ties between the EU and US have also deteriorated over trade and defense spending.

After the establishment of a civilian government under the leadership of Prime Minister Prayut Chan-Ocha in June 2019, the EU changed its attitude towards Thailand. In October last year, the Foreign Affairs Council decided to broaden its engagement with Thailand to prepare for the signing of the Partnership and Cooperation Agreement as well as to resume the negotiations of the Free Trade Agreement between Thailand and the EU. On its part, Thailand cited three principles on the basis of mutual respect, mutual trust and mutual benefits in forging stronger ties with the EU.

Relations between Thailand and the EU are headed towards a good ending. Thailand's experience in engaging the EU to prevent illegal, unregulated, and unreported (IUU) fishing has been praised by the EU and ASEAN. At the ASEAN Summit last year, the grouping's leaders agreed to set up a regional network on anti-IUU, so that other ASEAN members, facing similar problems, could learn from the Thai experience. Indeed, it was a rare diplomatic case between the ASEAN-EU relations that Thailand has turned things around from a bad apple to best practitioner, setting an example for others to follow.

17

Vietnam-EU Relations
A Success Story

Hoang Thi Ha

Vietnam-EU relationship is a success story in the EU's engagement with Southeast Asia. It has progressed from a donor-recipient relationship in the early 1990s, with Hanoi's heavy reliance on the EU's humanitarian and development assistance, into a robust and multifaceted partnership as both sides celebrate the 30th anniversary of their relations this year.

Vietnam's good bilateral ties with individual EU members provide a solid foundation for its relations with the organisation. Hanoi has established strategic partnerships with key EU member states, namely France, Germany, Italy, Spain, and the UK pre-Brexit, as well as comprehensive partnerships with Denmark, Hungary, and the Netherlands. Vietnam also maintains traditional friendship with the members that once belonged to the Cold War communist camp, namely the Czech Republic, Romania, Bulgaria, Hungary and Poland. Besides, the presence of large Vietnamese overseas communities in several EU countries — estimated at more than a million — provides a key conduit for extensive business and people-to-people links between both sides, and for promoting EU soft power among the Vietnamese people.

Vietnam-EU relations are embedded by a wide array of agreements that guide bilateral dialogue and cooperation, starting with the 1995 Cooperation Agreement between the EU and Vietnam. Under the Agreement, the EU undertook to support Vietnam's poverty alleviation and restructuring of its economy towards a market-based one. As bilateral cooperation grew and expanded, the Vietnam-EU Partnership and Cooperation Agreement (PCA) was signed in 2012, to enable "the comprehensive partnership on a more equal footing for mutual benefit, one that is commensurate with the new stature and strength of both the EU and Vietnam", as remarked by Vietnam's deputy foreign minister Bui Thanh Son. Since then, the relations have gone from strength to strength despite their normative and other disagreements.

Robust Economic Exchanges

Economics is the key driver of Vietnam-EU relations, especially seen from Hanoi. The EU is Vietnam's third largest trading partner and second biggest export market. Bilateral trade grew from US$12.6 billion in 2009 to US$56.4 billion in 2019, with Vietnam sustaining large trade surpluses according to the General Department of Vietnam Customs. The EU is also Vietnam's largest aid provider and one of the biggest foreign investors with the total stock of €6.1 billion as of 2017.

For the EU, Vietnam is its second largest trading partner in ASEAN, after Singapore. Vietnam's sizeable, young and vibrant population with a burgeoning middle class holds increasing attraction to EU businesses both as an investment destination and export market. Vietnam is also the second most open economy in ASEAN, plugged to an extensive network of bilateral and multilateral free trade agreements, with the share of trade in GDP at 208%. Hence, its potential to serve as a manufacturing hub and a gateway for EU exports to Southeast Asia and the wider region. As noted by the European Parliamentary Research Service last year, "For EU companies, Vietnam is a highly attractive place to do business, not just as a competitive production base with low labour costs and access to the dynamic Southeast Asian region, but also as a rapidly growing market for EU exports."

Bilateral economic relations will be given a strong boost upon the entry into force of the EU-Vietnam Free Trade Agreement (EVFTA) on 1 August 2020 and the EU-Vietnam Investment Protection Agreement (EVIPA). Signed in June 2019, these momentous agreements are viewed by Vietnam's Prime Minister Nguyen Xuan Phuc as "two expressways that connect Vietnam and the EU with greater speed and scale" and "bring their partnership to strategic heights". Upon the EVFTA's entry into force, 71% of Vietnam's exports will enter the EU market duty-free, and the coverage will expand to 99% in the next seven years. Meanwhile, 65% of EU exports to Vietnam will be tariff-free immediately and the remaining tariffs will be phased out in the next 10 years. According to projections by Vietnam's Ministry of Investment and Planning, the EVFTA will contribute a 2.18–3.23% growth to the country's GDP for the 2019–2023 period, 4.57–5.30% for 2024–2028, and 7.07–7.72% for 2029–2033.

In terms of investment, it is expected that the agreements will stimulate FDI inflows not only from the EU but also other countries' firms which see relocation of their manufacturing base to Vietnam as a natural pathway to enjoy duty-free exports to the EU. Furthermore, the key sectors of EU investments are industrial processing and manufacturing, which are in line with Vietnam's endeavour to restructure its economy towards a strong manufacturing base and step up its position in the value chains. With more quality investment from the EU, more local Vietnamese small and medium enterprises (SMEs) are hoping to be able to participate in EU firms' global supply networks.

Beyond the foreign trade perspective, the EVFTA is expected to have significant long-term impact on Vietnam's economic restructuring and governance reform. It is the first high-quality FTA signed between the EU and a developing country in Asia-Pacific, covering not only trade in goods, services, and investment, but also new-generation FTA provisions such as government procurement, state-owned enterprises, intellectual property, environment and labour standards. For example, under the agreement, EU firms will be able to compete for Vietnamese public procurement contracts at the central level, and sub-central level in Hanoi and Ho Chi Minh City. Many Vietnamese businesses see in the agreement both pressures and incentives to improve their competitiveness, quality and productivity, not only to meet EU high standards required for its market access but also to compete with EU products and services right in the Vietnamese market.

In fact, the agreements both reflect and influence the Vietnamese government's strategy of leveraging free trade agreements to incentivise and energise its economic restructuring towards greater transparency, efficiency, and the rule of law. During the negotiation process on the two agreements, Vietnam has undertaken legal and regulatory reforms to bring them in line with liberalisation commitments. In the agriculture sector which constitutes a large share of exports to the EU, Vietnam has amended or enacted at least four legal codes on fisheries, crop production, animal husbandry and forestry, together with implementing legislation, during 2017–2018. According to the WTO Centre of the Vietnam Chamber of Commerce and Industry (VCCI), 80% of Vietnam's legal and regulatory framework has been in line with the EVFTA on intellectual property, public procurement, transparency, customs, and investment protection. Going forward, implementation and enforcement of these legislations are of paramount importance.

Managing Normative Differences

Vietnam-EU relations are not without difficult issues, given their differences in political systems, governance standards and development levels. Vietnam is therefore no exception among some ASEAN member countries that have encountered difficulties with the EU over either political problems (Cambodia and Myanmar) or sustainability concerns (Indonesia and Malaysia). The European Parliament issued resolutions criticising Vietnam's human rights record in three straight years from 2016 to 2018. Meanwhile, the EU-imposed "yellow card" status that restricts Vietnam's seafood exports to the EU remains in place since 2017.

It is, however, noteworthy that Vietnam and the EU have forged significant economic and strategic convergence that helps buffer some of these hard edges. Although human rights continues to be a problem in bilateral ties, both sides have developed mechanisms to manage this sensitive domain without affecting the overall relationship, including the annual Human Rights Dialogue that provides a platform for the EU to voice its concerns over human rights issues in Vietnam. The Vietnamese government has put business first in pushing forward economic relations with the EU while political-ideological reservations take a back seat. In the *State of Southeast Asia 2020* survey conducted by ISEAS-Yusof Ishak Institute, only 9.4% of Vietnamese respondents cited the incompatibility of political culture as the reason for their lack of trust in the EU.

The EU itself has also displayed dexterity and pragmatism in dealing with Hanoi on this issue. The European Commission has thus far maintained a low-key approach and tried to reconcile its normative drive with *realpolitik* so as not to undermine its economic and strategic interests with Vietnam. The eight-year long journey of the EVFTA and EVIPA, which were ratified by the European Parliament in February 2020, is a prime example of that pragmatism as economic considerations have been prioritised over human rights and sustainability concerns.

In addition, the EU's approach of leveraging its economic largesse to induce its labour and environmental standards in Vietnam has yielded some transformative effects. Last year both sides concluded the Voluntary Partnership Agreement (VPA) on Forest Law Enforcement, Governance and Trade, with the underlying rationale: Vietnam will have to act robustly and credibly against illegal logging to pave the way for its legal timber exports to the EU market. In another example, the imposition of the EU's "yellow card" has pressured Vietnam to implement a raft of measures since 2017, including amendment of the Law on Fisheries and rigorous enforcement activities to address the issue of illegal, unreported and unregulated (IUU) fishing.

Even on the sensitive issue of human rights, Hanoi has gone the extra mile politically so as to benefit economically from its partnership with the EU. It agreed to tie the fulfilment of its obligations under the PCA, including on human rights, to the implementation and/or suspension of the EVFTA and EVIPA. Another significant political concession that is linked to Vietnam's EVFTA commitments is on labour rights. Last year, it ratified the International Labour Organization (ILO) Convention 98 on the Right to Organise and Collective Bargaining, and enacted the new Labour Code recognising the right of employees to set up their own trade unions — a breakthrough that brings its labour legislation closer to international standards. However, implementation of this clause remains tricky since there are ambiguities subject to sub-law implementing legislation, for example on the minimum number of internal employees required for the registration of a representative organisation.

Partners for Peace and a Rules-based Order

Vietnam-EU security cooperation is emerging as the Vietnamese military actively diversifies its defence cooperation and participates in regional defence diplomacy, and the EU seeks to raise its strategic-security profile in Southeast Asia and beyond. The signing of the Framework Participation Agreement (FPA) in 2019 provides the basis for more concrete defence cooperation between Vietnam and the EU, including Vietnam's participation in EU crisis management and other capacity-building activities, and a bilateral defence policy dialogue.

Beyond defence cooperation, both sides share growing strategic convergence in upholding the regional rules-based order which is under stress due to the ongoing power shift associated with China's rise and US-China contestation. In the maritime domain, Vietnam finds in the EU a like-minded partner committed to the legal order for the seas and oceans, and in speaking out against activities in the South China Sea that are incompatible with international law, including the 1982 United Nations Convention on the Law of the Sea.

Furthermore, as one of ASEAN's most strategically outward-looking members, Hanoi supports the EU's role and engagement in the open and inclusive regional architecture. 67.8% of Vietnamese respondents in the above survey supported opening of the Regional Comprehensive Economic Partnership (RCEP) to the EU, and 92.8% supported ASEAN-EU inter-regional FTA. They also picked the EU as their second top choice in championing the global free trade agenda, maintaining the rules-based order and upholding international law.

However, this high level of trust has yet to be translated into the EU's security footprint and strategic influence in the region. Despite Vietnam's pledge of support, the EU's bid to join the ASEAN Defence Ministers Meeting Plus (ADMM-Plus) and the East Asia Summit (EAS) remains at a standstill, given the lack of consensus and little appetite within ASEAN to open up the two platforms to the EU. Vietnam's pledge of support appears to be commercially driven by the overriding imperative to secure the EU's backing of the EVFTA, rather than by the recognition of the

EU as a full-fledged security actor in its own right. In the above survey, among those Vietnamese respondents who did not have confidence in the EU, 56.6% were concerned over the EU's distraction with its internal affairs, and 30.2% over its limited capacity or political will to exercise global leadership. Another survey by Reuben Wong suggested that many in Indonesia, Singapore and Vietnam still perceived the EU as a "one-dimensional actor in the region, strong in economic capacity, but weak in the political and military realms". As the EU seeks to enhance its strategic-security profile in the region, it must overcome not only its internal constraints but also this prevailing Southeast Asian perception.

Conclusion

The development of Vietnam-EU relations over the past three decades has been remarkable not only because of the growing convergence of common interests, but also by a shared determination to turn their normative disagreements into cooperative platforms. The EU has finely walked the line between upholding its values and making constructive pathways forward, setting its sight on the key objectives of supporting Vietnam's economic restructuring, environmental protection and sustainable management of natural resources. The Vietnamese government has reciprocated with a sustained and proven commitment to opening-up and economic reform. Hanoi also managed to adeptly deal with the many layers of EU decision-making, its bureaucratic complexities, and its tensions between supra-nationality and inter-governmentality.

Entering its fourth decade, Vietnam-EU relations are on the cusp of a new chapter, one that is characterised by higher standards, fairer competition, and more equal partnership. To that end, challenges abound for Vietnam as its government has to press ahead with more structural reforms to be in alignment with international standards. Vietnamese enterprises, while facing greater competition from EU products in their home market, will need to increase their local content, adjust production process, and improve product quality, to meet EU stringent requirements on rules of origin, labour and environment compliance. Politically, disagreements over human rights issues will arise from time to time, with the European Parliament at the forefront in this domain. Hopefully, the proven benefits of cooperation and the deep reservoir of mutual trust and understanding accumulated over the past decades will help both sides navigate their partnership towards new heights and successes.

Part Four

Enhanced Cooperation into the Future

18

The ASEAN-EU Comprehensive Air Transport Agreement (CATA)
Potential and Reality

Alan Khee-Jin Tan

Overview

In February 2014, transport and aviation officials from the Association of Southeast Asian Nations (ASEAN) and the European Union (EU) convened a landmark Aviation Summit on the side-lines of the Singapore Air Show. Their aim was to discuss a possible comprehensive air transport agreement (CATA) between both sides that would raise aviation relations to a new level. A Joint Declaration on EU-ASEAN Aviation Co-operation was adopted at the Summit, laying out the mutual commitment to strengthen aviation relations between both regions.

In June 2016, the European Commission received authorisation from its member states to commence negotiations with ASEAN on the CATA. The first round of negotiations began in Brussels in October 2016, and a total of eight rounds have since been held. At the time of writing (March 2020), the CATA is effectively ready for adoption, but is held up because one ASEAN state — Malaysia — remains cautious over its provisions on fair competition.

At first glance, the prospects for an ASEAN-EU "bloc-to-bloc" agreement are promising: it will be the first agreement worldwide to spell out an "open skies" arrangement between two major regional trading blocs. This could have a huge liberalising impact by providing unlimited traffic rights and market access for both regions' airlines into each other's respective territories, along with other benefits. Indeed, with 28 (though now 27 with the UK's departure) and 10 countries respectively and a combined population of over a billion, the EU and ASEAN economies stand to gain significantly from the CATA.

One impetus for the CATA is the common wish on both sides to stem the loss of air traffic to the so-called "sixth freedom" carriers. These are the third country airlines like Emirates, Etihad, Qatar Airways and Turkish Airlines that operate out of airport mega-hubs located strategically in between the two regions. They thus offer convenient one-stop operations for passengers travelling between ASEAN and the EU, and are estimated to capture almost half of the total passengers in this market.

ASEAN-EU Market Dynamics

Unlimited third/fourth freedom rights

One key liberalizing feature in the CATA will be the complete relaxation of the third and fourth freedom rights on a bloc-to-bloc basis. Hence, market access in the form of direct, non-stop flights between the two regions operated by airlines designated by both sides will become unlimited in capacity, frequency and aircraft type. This will greatly improve on the existing bilateral air services agreements between individual states on both sides, some of which still restrict the capacity that can be operated on certain routes.

With the CATA, major hub-to-hub operations between, say, Singapore, Bangkok, Jakarta and Kuala Lumpur (on the ASEAN side) and Frankfurt, Paris, Amsterdam and Madrid (on the EU side) will likely see increased flight frequencies, along with more competition and choice for passengers and lower ticket prices.

In theory, this should enhance the ASEAN and EU carriers' competitiveness as against the mid-point sixth freedom carriers.

The reality, however, is that the ASEAN and EU carriers will continue to face tremendous competition from the Gulf and Turkish carriers. This is because these sixth freedom carriers collect passenger "feed" from other regions such as Northeast Asia, North America and Africa as well. As such, their operations benefit from superior geography and greater economies of scale in terms of being able to channel passengers from a greater number of markets through their respective hubs. This is particularly important for filling up aircraft on the thinner routes involving smaller cities.

What this means is that the CATA's promise of unlimited third/fourth freedom capacity between ASEAN and the EU may not help much to justify direct, non-stop flights between ASEAN and the smaller non-hub EU cities such as Bordeaux, Lisbon, Dublin, Krakow or Zagreb. The problem for these operations is not the lack of traffic rights but simply, the absence of a large enough market to fill up aircraft and generate sufficient yield.

The same applies for direct flights between the EU and ASEAN cities such as Bali, Phuket, Manila, Hanoi or Yangon. By dint of their superior geography and operating economics, the Gulf and Turkish sixth-freedom carriers are much better-positioned to exploit their "hub-and-spokes" advantage and collect greater passenger "feed" from across all regions. Indeed, all the above-named cities are already connected by one or more of these sixth freedom carriers through their respective hubs.

Consequently, an ASEAN-EU CATA that offers unlimited third/fourth freedom capacity is likely to boost only the hub-to-hub operations between both regions. The thinner routes will continue to be hard to fill. Even for hub routes, there is unlikely to be a significant increase in actual traffic carried. With some exceptions like Singapore-Paris, most direct ASEAN-EU trunk routes already enjoy unlimited or near-unlimited capacity under the existing bilateral agreements. For instance, Singapore and Malaysian carriers have had unlimited rights into London Heathrow and all UK points since 2007; the real problem here is the lack of landing and take-off slots at Heathrow which the CATA does not fix!

Elsewhere, unlimited or generous capacity for ASEAN carriers to fly to the likes of Brussels, Berlin or Barcelona already exist, but is largely unutilised due to the lack of a market for regular and profitable operations. Similarly, the EU carriers have more than enough capacity into points such as Kuala Lumpur, Yangon, Hanoi, Phnom Penh and Jakarta but these have also been unprofitable. Overall, unlimited capacity into points such as Paris, Athens and Manila that remain restricted by the relevant bilateral agreements might be welcomed but elsewhere, unlimited traffic rights *alone* will not help the ASEAN and EU carriers fill up their flights profitably, especially on the thinner non-hub routes.

Limited fifth freedom rights

The proposed CATA will also seek to relax fifth freedom operations. These enable the airlines to mount itineraries with additional stops outside of the EU or ASEAN, e.g. Air France operating Paris — Mumbai — Singapore, or Paris — Singapore — Sydney, with the ability to take on and disembark traffic in all sectors in both directions. Conversely, ASEAN carriers like Singapore Airlines could mount Singapore — Colombo — Frankfurt or Singapore — Amsterdam — New York, again with traffic rights between Colombo and Frankfurt, and Amsterdam and New York.

Such fifth freedom rights already exist in a number of the current bilateral agreements, although their daily or weekly capacity is often restricted. Singapore Airlines, for instance, exercises beyond-Germany fifth freedom rights for its daily

Singapore — Frankfurt — New York (JFK) operations, with traffic pick-up rights between Frankfurt and New York in both directions. The capacity is restricted by Germany to only 7 weekly flights, with the objective of protecting Lufthansa's competitiveness on the Frankfurt — New York route.

Unsurprisingly, relaxing beyond-EU fifth freedom rights emerged as the most contentious aspect of the CATA market access negotiations. This was because the highly lucrative trans-Atlantic market to the US would be impacted if ASEAN carriers were liberally permitted to carry traffic between Europe and the US. The EU airlines and their member states have always guarded this market jealously, and the ASEAN states would have to offer equally lucrative benefits in exchange.

Here, the logical beyond-ASEAN market to barter would have been Australia and New Zealand. Yet, the EU carriers that have attempted this route in the past have mostly pulled out due to the high operating costs and severe competition. In fact, British Airways remains the only EU carrier still operating fifth freedom flights to Australia (Sydney) from London via Singapore. Even then, the competition is stiff due to over-capacity in this sector. Hence, ASEAN could not offer beyond-ASEAN rights to Australia and New Zealand as a bargaining chip simply because the EU carriers already have more capacity on these routes than they need under the current bilateral arrangements.

After protracted negotiations, both sides have now reached agreement for fifth freedom rights. The negotiators adopted the EU proposal that seven weekly fifth freedom flights would be allowed for each ASEAN-EU country pair, with an additional seven weekly flights being permitted if no airline from the other side operates the route. Thus, for instance, Singapore carriers would have seven weekly fifth freedom flights through *each* of the EU's 27 member states, such as Singapore — Lisbon — Sao Paolo (seven weekly out of Portugal) and Singapore — Paris — Boston (seven weekly out of France).

An additional seven weekly flights would be permitted between any points in Portugal (or France) and say, a US point, if those routes are not otherwise served by an EU carrier. In turn, Lufthansa would have seven weekly fifth freedom rights from any point in Germany to Singapore and onward to any point in Australia or elsewhere, with an additional seven weekly flights through Singapore to any other point that is not served by any ASEAN carrier.

ASEAN's Incomplete Single Market

Meanwhile, there remains a fundamental problem in the fact that ASEAN has yet to forge a true single or common aviation market, in the manner that the EU has. Thus, airlines from ASEAN can only be designated by their respective home states, while EU carriers can be designated by all their member states. As such, the ASEAN-EU CATA will practically mean that an ASEAN airline will be able to operate third/fourth freedom flights to EU points *only from its home national territory* (and not from other ASEAN points — this would have been the "seventh freedom" right that the ASEAN states are not yet prepared to grant each other).

Conversely, all EU-designated airlines can fly to all ASEAN points from any number of points across the EU, for the simple reason that the EU "backyard" is now a unified one. This presents a significant market imbalance that disadvantages the ASEAN carriers in the longer term. Moreover, EU airlines can now merge among themselves the way Air France-KLM, British Airways-Iberia and Lufthansa-SWISS-Austrian have done pursuant to the community ownership regime in the EU. This remains impossible for the ASEAN airlines whose designating states still uphold the traditional national ownership and control rules. All these market imbalances can be corrected only if the ASEAN states begin treating their own backyard as a true single market but this will take years to realise.

The result is that for the immediate future, an ASEAN-EU CATA with open or unlimited third/fourth freedom capacity will benefit the EU airlines more in terms of market networks and penetration. Yet, the pragmatic ASEAN position is that it is unrealistic to wait for its own internal market to be completed first before engaging with external trading partners. This is why ASEAN had gone ahead to adopt a similar air transport agreement with China in 2010, despite all the imbalances described above. Hence, Chinese airlines can now fly from all of China to all of ASEAN, while ASEAN airlines can fly to all of China *only from points in their home states.*

The lack of a united negotiating stand is also partly why ASEAN could not convince the Chinese to allow fifth freedom rights through the major cities of Beijing, Shanghai and Guangzhou, settling instead for a limited regime of fifth freedom rights through a finite list of pre-determined cities. Fundamentally, apart from lacking a supranational institution like the European Commission to prioritize the regional over national interests, the problem with ASEAN is that the individual member states' levels of development are too disparate. As a result, ASEAN's negotiations with the EU were inevitably constrained by the same aero-political asymmetries that it encountered with China.

Conclusion

Ultimately, there is probably not much that an ASEAN-EU CATA with unlimited third/fourth freedom capacity can do to stem the continuing bleeding of traffic to sixth freedom carriers. Meanwhile, the liberalised fifth freedom regime promised by the CATA will likely advantage the ASEAN carriers more, given the more lucrative trans-Atlantic opportunities open to them. The lack of a true internal market in ASEAN means that only the EU carriers will be able to connect any EU point with any ASEAN point effectively. This is because the EU carriers have a true common market and can begin and end their flights at any EU point, while enjoying the facility of outright mergers between or among them. None of these advantages are available to the ASEAN carriers, meaning that in the final analysis, an ASEAN-EU CATA is likely to favour the EU carriers more, at least in the shorter term.

Postscript

Since this chapter was written, the COVID-19 pandemic has struck worldwide, inflicting severe human health and economic costs as well as unprecedented losses to the global aviation industry. With states sealing their borders and demand for air travel plummeting, the airline association IATA (International Air Transport Association) has estimated that the crisis will cause airline passenger revenues to drop by USD314 billion in 2020, a 55% decline from 2019. Some airlines have collapsed, while others have turned to their governments for massive financial support, even as they carry out relief flights to bring home stranded passengers as well as essential cargoes such as medical and protective equipment.

How does that change the prospects for the ASEAN-EU CATA? The post-pandemic aviation world is likely to see an upsurge in protectionism for struggling airlines, including in ASEAN and the EU. State aid and subsidies will become normalised as states seek to keep their airlines afloat. States are also likely to enforce strict ownership and control rules as more airlines become nationalised or deemed as ultra-strategic assets. In such an environment, there could be diminished appetite for further market liberalisation and competition, at least in the short term. In the long run, though, airlines will need liberalised markets for recovery, and the ASEAN-EU CATA will likely be adopted once the pandemic passes and demand rebounds.

19

The European Union and ASEAN
Deepening Cooperation in Human Security

Mely Caballero-Anthony

Many scholars and analysts have always tried to draw a distinction in the nature of regional integration between the European Union (EU) and ASEAN. Other than the vast differences in socio-cultural attributes, the level of institutionalisation between these two regional organisations has been cited as one important factor that explains why the speed and depth of integration is faster in one than the other. Yet, if one were to highlight the similarities between EU and ASEAN in their respective pursuit of regional peace and security, a key feature that stands out is the emphasis on common and cooperative security to deal with a range of regional/ global security and developmental challenges.

The EU's emphasis on "prosperity, people and planet" and ASEAN's vision of "an ASEAN Community that is inclusive, sustainable, resilient and dynamic" speak of a shared vision of ensuring people's comprehensive security against a rapidly changing global environment beset with multifaceted challenges. With ever growing connectivity brought on by globalisation, we now live in a world of heightened anxiety where a security issue in one state can easily become a security problem for its neighbours and the wider region. These issues can stem from a range of transborder problems such as an outbreak of an epidemic like SARS and COVID-19, growing number of population displacement caused by devastating natural disasters and ethnic conflicts, higher risks of widespread hunger and malnutrition from water and food scarcity, and the other threats from climate change. Given the transnationality of these issues, the strategies to ensure human security through the provision of regional or global public goods require no less than closer international and multilateral cooperation. In this regard, a strong ASEAN-EU partnership becomes an important pillar in advancing multilateral cooperation on human security.

Writing on global public goods, Inge Kaul, et al. pointed out that as the fate of many nations becomes increasingly intertwined, the approach of shared responsibility allows for "institutions, mechanisms and outcomes that provide quasi universal benefits, covering a group of countries, several population groups that [extend] to both current and future generations".[1] Seen against this approach, there is therefore much that ASEAN and the EU can do to forge closer partnership to achieve comprehensive security.

Deepening ASEAN-EU Cooperation

ASEAN-EU cooperation has existed formally since 1977. The cooperation was significantly reinforced in the 2017 Nuremberg Declaration calling for combatting the effects of greenhouse gas emissions, as well as in "addressing the growing concern of the spread of infectious diseases such as HIV/AIDS, SARS, disaster management, increasing people-to-people contact though cultural exchanges, interfaith dialogue, etc., and expanding cooperation in S&T, education, arts and culture, etc.".[2]

More recently, a more defined partnership agenda was crafted that highlights a number of issues for enhanced

---

[1] I. Kaul, I. Grunberg and M.A. Stern (eds.), *Global Public Goods*. Oxford University Press, 1999.
[2] S. Kumar, "The EU-ASEAN Socio-Cultural Cooperation", 2019.

cooperation between ASEAN and the EU. Among these are: education to "harmonise higher education frameworks in ASEAN through the mutual recognition of qualifications..." through the European Union Support to Higher Education in the ASEAN Region (EU SHARE) programme; migration to "(contribute) to improving labour conditions for migrant women in Southeast Asia through the Safe and Fair programme"; biodiversity to support the preservation of the region's biological diversity as well as the management of protected areas through the Biodiversity Conservation and Management of Protected Areas in ASEAN (BCAMP); responsible land use and forestry in relation to Peatlands through the Sustainable Use of Peatland and Haze Mitigation in ASEAN (SUPA) programme; and most recently, disaster resilience to increase the region's resilience to disasters through the "Integrated Programme in Enhancing the Capacity of AHA Centre and ASEAN Emergency Response Mechanisms (EU Support to AHA Centre)".[3]

These issue-areas are extremely important particularly for ASEAN which has placed a lot of emphasis on building resilience to enhance the capacity of its member states "to collectively respond and adapt to current challenges and emerging threats".[4] To be sure, the scope of ASEAN-EU multilateral cooperation can be as broad as it can get given the common interests and similar priorities of these two organisations.

Harnessing Common Visions, Common Interest and Similar Priorities

Against the long list of areas for enhancing inter-regional cooperation, this paper identifies three priority areas where enhanced

---

[3] European External Union, "'Backgrounder on EU-ASEAN Development Cooperation", 8 August 2019.
[4] ASEAN, *ASEAN Socio-Cultural Community Blueprint 2025,* Jakarta: ASEAN Secretariat, March 2016.

bilateral cooperation can best be advanced to meet the challenge of building resilience especially for ASEAN countries.

Climate change

The multi-faceted impact of climate is now being felt acutely in many parts of the world. As a threat multiplier, climate change already presents a number of grave challenges for human security ranging from extreme weather events that cause prolonged droughts affecting food and water security, to devastating natural disasters like cyclones and hurricanes which result in extensive destruction of properties, huge loss of lives and massive displacement of peoples. Many of these impacts are in fact also identified and already further established as drivers of conflict.

The EU established the European Environment Agency (EEA), a dedicated body, that specifically looks into environment-related issues including climate change. The EEA has facilitated a comprehensive approach that covers the necessary enabling factors for the implementation of regional climate actions at the national level. These include funding, technical and policy support tools, knowledge-sharing platforms, a meteorological services body, and research institutions.[5] Copernicus Climate Change Services, for example, was established to monitor and analyse weather and climatic data.

The EU also has a committed "LIFE" funding programme that can be tapped into for climate change adaptation and mitigation efforts. Through its Horizon 2020 programme, the EU has invested €80 billion in new, innovative and smart technology between 2014 and 2020, which among others has allowed it to conduct comprehensive assessments of climate adaptation gaps within member states.[6] The incorporation

---

[5] European Commission. "Strengthening Europe's Resilience to the Impacts of Climate Change", 2018.
[6] Ibid.

of research, and science and technology elements into the adaptation approach shows that EU is committed to finding its own solutions to the kinds of problems that were identified in the vulnerability assessments of climate change. Moreover, the EU has established an important mechanism for information exchange, Climate-ADAPT, that provides a web-based knowledge-exchange platform.[7]

The notable progress that the EU has achieved in climate change adaptation and the sharing of best practices through extensive web-based information exchange is indeed very useful to ASEAN in its own efforts in building regional adaptive capacity. There is much that ASEAN can learn from the EU's whole-of-Europe approach for effective regional climate change response and much that EU can also help ASEAN with developing its own capacity. For instance, aside from providing financial support, the EU can help ASEAN establish an ASEAN Climate Change Adaptation Centre, which like its EU Climate Change Data Centre can potentially provide valuable scientific data and projections on regional vulnerabilities to climate effects.

Food security and food safety

Food security and safety is another issue-area where ASEAN and the EU can work together. Apart from ensuring adequate supply and access to food commodities, a growing threat faced by ASEAN today is the increasing complexity of addressing food-borne diseases or FBDs. Two key factors contributing to this growing complexity, are: i) the over-use of antibiotics in food production, for growth purposes, which is hastening the pace at which some bacteria are adapting to antibiotics meant to cure them, i.e. antimicrobial resistance (AMR), and ii) the

---

[7] European Commission and the European Environment Agency. "European Climate Adaptation Platform".

fragmentation of food supply chains, making it harder to keep track of/or identify diseases sources as production processes are geographically dispersed across multiple countries.

A potential opportunity for collaboration is in improving the risk assessment standards in the region, moving from a hazards-based approach to a risk-based approach.[8] It has been observed during the 2016 EU-ASEAN Forum on Food Safety that while ASEAN has its own ASEAN Food Safety Regulatory Framework and an ASEAN Risk Assessment Centre (ARAC) at the regional level, a clear imperative moving forward is to bring this down to the national level.[9] The EU has the potential to share its lessons on how it has contributed to helping its member states improve their own national capacities for disease monitoring and tracking.

Health security

There is much that the EU and ASEAN can do to advance health security in a rapidly changing global environment. One of these is in the critical area of pandemic preparedness, especially against current developments in relation to the transborder spread of COVID-19. The global public health emergency caused by this virus has once again underscored the importance of putting public health in regional and global security agenda. Aside from the grave threats to human health, global epidemics can lead to

---

[8] Jose Ma. Luis Montesclaros, Mely Caballero-Anthony and Joergen Schlundt, "Food Safety in ASEAN: Pitfalls of Complacency", *RSIS Commentaries*, 7 September 2018. Accessed 6 March 2020. See also, Jose Ma. Montesclaros, Mely Caballero-Anthony and Joergen Schlundt, "Supporting the Genome Microbial Identifier and Whole Genome Sequencing in Addressing Food-Borne Diseases in ASEAN," *RSIS Policy Report*, October 2018. Singapore: S. Rajaratnam School of International Studies, Nanyang Technological University, Singapore, 2018.

[9] Joergen Schlundt. "ASEAN Food Safety Developments: Continued Harmonization Efforts." The EU-ASEAN Forum on Food Safety. Kuala Lumpur, Malaysia: European Union, EU-Malaysia Chamber of Commerce and Industry (EU-MCCI), and Support for European Business in South East Asia Markets Malaysia Component (SEBSEAM-M).

plunging stock markets and sudden economic downturns and consequently, massive job losses and economic displacement for hundreds of people. Prolonged health crises and sudden economic downturns also generate political instability as issues of legitimacy and effectiveness to govern start to fester. Moreover, epidemics heighten psycho-social stresses and disorders, often fuelled by misinformation and misperceptions.[10]

The EU and ASEAN can strengthen international, multilateral cooperation in pandemic preparedness and response. Given the current concern of the global spread of COVID-19, it is critical for countries to have the capacity to *prevent*, *detect*, and *respond* to outbreaks of infectious diseases that threaten regional and global security. The importance of building multi-level capacity in pandemic preparedness cannot be understated. As noted in the report of the Global Health Security Conference in 2018, 'every country must have a detection network, people who can respond effectively (trained epidemiologists), information systems to observe signals and discrepancies, and rapid response teams that operate out of emergency operation centres.'

With the wide disparity in public health systems in ASEAN and the varying levels of pandemic preparedness among its members, the EU and ASEAN can work together to enhance the capacity of countries to strengthen their own disease surveillance and reporting mechanisms, as well as help build proper laboratories and diagnostic facilities including testing-kits. More cooperation can also be done in developing vaccines and providing access to them and other medicines, and perhaps even exploring the possibility of building a regional stockpile as part of pandemic preparedness.

---

[10] Mely Caballero-Anthony, "SARS in Asia: Crisis, vulnerabilities, and regional responses." *Asian Survey*, 45(3), 2005, 475–495. See also, Caballero-Anthony, "The Wuhan Virus Pandemic: What Next?" *RSIS Commentaries*, February 2020.

In sum, the kinds of transnational threats to human security present an urgent and compelling argument for global action. Many of these challenges lend themselves to international cooperation. It is in this arena where enhanced EU-ASEAN partnership can provide not only a strong pillar but also significant boost to multilateral cooperation.

References

ASEAN (2016). *ASEAN Socio-Cultural Community Blueprint 2025*. Jakarta: ASEAN Secretariat, March. Accessed 4 March 2020, https://asean.org/storage/2016/01/ASCC-Blueprint-2025.pdf.

Caballero-Anthony, M. (2020). "The Wuhan Virus Pandemic: What Next?" *RSIS Commentaries*. Accessed 6 March 2020, https://www.rsis.edu.sg/rsis-publication/nts/the-wuhan-virus-pandemic-what-next/#.XmHRGagzbb0.

Caballero-Anthony, M. (2005). "SARS in Asia: crisis, vulnerabilities, and regional responses." *Asian Survey*, 45(3), 475-495. Accessed 6 March 2020, https://as.ucpress.edu/content/45/3/475.

Caballero-Anthony, M., Montesclaros, J.M.L., and Sembiring, M. (2019). "Addressing Disaster Risk, Climate Change, and Food Security through Successful Structural and Non-Structural Measures in Country Adaptation Roadmaps," in Anbumozhi, V., Gross, J. and Wesiak, S. (Eds)., *Volume 2: Advancing Disaster Resilience and Climate Change Adaptation: Roadmaps and Options for Implementation*. Jakarta: Economic Research Institute for ASEAN and East Asia (ERIA). Accessed 6 March 2020, https://www.eria.org/publications/towards-a-resilient-asean-volume-2-advancing-disaster-resilience-and-climate-change-adaptation-roadmap-and-options-for-implementation/.

European Commission and the European Environment Agency. "European Climate Adaptation Platform". Accessed 4 March 2020. https://climate-adapt.eea.europa.eu/.

European Commission (2018). "Strengthening Europe's Resilience to the Impacts of Climate Change." Accessed 6 March 2020. https://ec.europa.eu/clima/sites/clima/files/docs/eu_strategy_en.pdf.

European External Union (2019). *Backgrounder on EU-ASEAN Development Cooperation*. 8 August 2019. Accessed 4 March 2020, https://eeas.europa.eu/headquarters/headquarters-homepage/66301/node/66301_th.

Kaul, Inge I. Grunberg and M.A. Stern (eds), *Global Public Goods*. Oxford University Press, 1999. Accessed 6 March 2019, https://www.oxfordscholarship.com/view/10.1093/0195130529.001.0001/acprof-9780195130522.

Kumar, S. (2019). "The EU-ASEAN Socio-Cultural Cooperation," in *EU-ASEAN Relations: Perspectives from Malaysia*. Kuala Lumpur, Malaysia: Asia-Europe Institute: 27-38. Accessed 4 March 2020, https://aei.um.edu.my/the-eu-asean-socio-cultural-cooperation.

Montesclaros, J.M.L., Caballero-Anthony, M. and Schlundt, J. (2018). "Supporting the Genome Microbial Identifier and Whole Genome Sequencing in Addressing Food-Borne Diseases in ASEAN." *RSIS Policy Report*. Singapore: S. Rajaratnam School of International Studies, Nanyang Technological University Singapore, October. Accessed 4 March 2020, https://www.rsis.edu.sg/wp-content/uploads/2018/11/PR181121_Supporting-the-Genome-Microbial-Identifier-and-Whole-Genome.pdf.

Montesclaros, J.M.L., Caballero-Anthony, M. and Schlundt, J. (2018). "Food Safety in ASEAN: Pitfalls of Complacency." *RSIS Commentaries*, September. Accessed 6 March 2020, https://www.rsis.edu.sg/rsis-publication/nts/co18146-food-safety-in-asean-pitfalls-of-complacency/#.XmHP6agzbb0.

Schlundt, J. (2016). "ASEAN Food Safety Developments: Continued Harmonization Efforts." The EU-ASEAN Forum on Food Safety. Kuala Lumpur, Malaysia: European Union, EU-Malaysia Chamber of Commerce and Industry (EU-MCCI), and Support for European Business in South East Asia Markets Malaysia Component (SEBSEAM-M). Accessed 4 March 2020, http://www.eu-aseanforum.com/images/ASEAN-Food-Safety-Developments-white-paper-2016.pdf.

20

ASEAN-EU Trade Talks
Friends in Need

Jaya Ratnam

COVID-19 has severely disrupted the societies and economies of ASEAN and the EU. In its wake, the pandemic will fundamentally re-structure economies as well as how countries and regions engage each other, whether for trade or travel. These trends were already in play, but the pandemic will accelerate them. COVID 19 has broadened and sharpened the geo-political competition compounding the uncertainties and risks we both face. In its aftermath, the crisis will hothouse new structures, rules and norms, whether by design or unintended, which will shape our collective future.

ASEAN and the EU will be amongst those affected by these shifting sands. Both bring together and represent member states deeply dependent on a functioning rules-based international order. The EU may be larger and more integrated than the far more diverse ASEAN, but when faced with such multiple enveloping pressures, we are all just as exposed and vulnerable. ASEAN and the EU will be far worse off in such a troubled world, where cooperation becomes situational and transactional. Even for EU Member States, at the height of the pandemic, Schengen borders were unilaterally shut and exports of vital supplies, including medical and food, were curtailed even amongst themselves.

Rebooting the Relationship

Dealing with COVID-19 offers an opening to reset the ASEAN-EU relationship. As our economies reopen, the need for open economies, common standards and rules for a level playing field and institutions to effectively govern them as a driver for recovery has never been stronger. Should we work together our combined weight makes us a force to contend with, especially at a juncture when geopolitical competition is straining multilateralism.

Yet, the ASEAN-EU story so far has been a cautionary tale of missed opportunities. The travails of the emblematic region-to-region free trade agreement between ASEAN and the EU Free Trade Agreement (ASEAN-EU FTA) — first launched in 2007, set aside in 2009, relaunched in 2017 and now in a form of "negotiation purgatory" — has been well documented.

There is enough blame to share. Bilateral agendas, have overshadowed the larger region-to-region relationship. Unsurprisingly, the ASEAN-EU relationships has consistently under-performed the sum of its parts. It will continue to do so, unless we take a strategic decision to change course and the way we deal with each other.

Where Do We Go from Here?

Restoring confidence and trust will be crucial. We are all emerging from our shells far more insecure and inward looking; far less trusting of systems and each other. Protectionist pressures are growing, especially to make more permanent the unprecedented level of state support for the economies.

This is inevitable as countries fight for a slice of a shrinking economic pie. Shattered supply chains will be reformed, with pressures to become more localised and regionalised. ASEAN and the EU should work together to address this. By focusing on our comparative advantages, we can build complementarity and grow the economic pie.

Reviving and repurposing our two landmark cross regional initiatives — the ASEAN-EU FTA and ASEAN EU Comprehensive Air Transport Agreement (CATA) — could be a basis for a definitive cross-regional response to the crisis. Trade and travel connectivity are two sides of the same coin when working for restoration of global supply chains and open markets. Such cross regional agreements could offer a way forward addressing the central issue — it is not whether supply chains are local or global but whether it is resilient and reliable. A resilient supply chain would require diversification and inter-dependence — specific areas which the ASEAN-EU FTA and ASEAN-EU CATA can be tailored to address.

A return to the EU's preferred approach of "connect the dots" for an ASEAN-EU FTA — securing bilateral agreements with selected ASEAN countries before embarking on a regional enterprise — does not match what the moment demands. There has been some success in recent years; EU-Singapore FTA in 2019 followed by EU-Vietnam this year accounting for around 45% of the EU's total ASEAN trade. The EU should double down on its efforts to conclude similar agreements with Indonesia, Malaysia and Thailand.

However, these do not, and should not preclude the EU from concurrently actively pursuing a region-to-region agreement. ASEAN Member States have negotiated bilateral trade agreements with key regional partners concurrently with a regional FTA. Selective EU engagement of ASEAN MS without an over-arching effort at regional level does little for ASEAN centrality and ASEAN's value as a strategic partner for EU.

The EU is ASEAN's second largest trading partner and largest source of FDI. The EU-ASEAN Business Council highlighted that " …. (the) *European manufacturing in ASEAN today…. (m)uch of it is to serve local, regional or Asian markets as opposed to global markets. Changes were happening pre-pandemic, with more manufacturers looking to move production for non-Chinese markets to elsewhere, and ASEAN, particularly Vietnam, was becoming a significant beneficiary of that trend. If anything, the COVID-19 pandemic should accelerate that movement, and those ASEAN markets that have better international trade access through various trade agreements and welcoming FDI support programmes will undoubtedly be better placed to act on that."*

An ASEAN-EU regional agreement could be re-scoped to complement and build on — not replicate — the bilateral efforts. We could focus on two issues that both sides place importance, and will be central to our post-Covid 19 recovery plans — the sustainability and digital agenda. Even with COVID 19, the EU has affirmed its commitment to the "Green Deal" which is an ambitious and comprehensive effort to achieve its climate neutral goal by 2050. The success of the Green Deal is ultimately tied to EU's ability to strenghten global climate action, and support other partners who need it to achieve their Paris goals. It is important that it is aligned with principles and provisions of the Paris Agreement, respects WTO rules, facilitates trade and avoids raising new barriers to international trade. ASEAN becomes an obvious partner for the EU, and trade aspects of sustainability agenda could be addressed in regional FTA.

ASEAN and EU have similar stakes in the effective implementation of the Paris Accords. Securing cross regional commitment on trade aspects could serve as basis for global outcomes, especially in areas such as waste management, circular economy, water resources management, green cities, ocean governance, marine litter and plastics, where we can work together by bringing in technological and digital solutions. The Enhanced Regional EU-ASEAN Dialogue Instrument (E-READI) will be critical to translating commitments into reality. In turn, this could also provide the setting for mutually beneficial package on the common regional certification to support sustainability goals, especially but not limited to palm oil, perhaps taking inspiration from the EU's bilateral agreements on Forest Law, Governance and Trade (FLEGT) to address illegal logging and associated trade.

ASEAN and the EU also share common interests in designing common rules for the digital realm. The global trading system has become intertwined and dependent on networks and platforms to ensure smooth flow of data. A clear outcome from the pandemic is to accelerate the importance and centrality of digital trade in coming years. A McKinsey study shows that we have seen the equivalent of five years of consumer and business digital adoption in just eight weeks since the COVID-19 pandemic started. At the same time, competing rules will raise cost, and fragmented markets weigh down our ability to take advantage of the opportunities it offers to re-build in a post COVID world.

ASEAN's digital ambitions are laid out in the AEC Blueprint 2025, Masterplan on ASEAN Connectivity 2025, and the e-ASEAN Framework Agreement. To realise ASEAN's ambitions, the need for common standards, mutual recognition and interoperability is obvious, and the EU is the good partner for ASEAN, given its experience with General Data Protection Regulation (GDPR) and as co-convener of the Joint Statement Initiative on E-Commerce, which is negotiating a plurilateral agreement on digital trade. Singapore, and other like-minded countries, including Chile and New Zealand have concluded Digital Economy Partnership Agreement. There should be sufficient scope for a cross regional initiative to support these bilateral and plurilateral efforts.

Conclusion of the ASEAN-EU Comprehensive Air Transport Agreement takes on fresh if unintended significance in post COVID 19 environments. Air travel will be transformed by the pandemic. Its restoration will be critical to keep up the cross regional trade supply chains and investment flows. At the height of pandemic, while passenger traffic plummeted, air transport kept crucial supply chains functioning, including for pharmaceuticals and food. An ASEAN-EU CATA would provide a liberal and holistic framework to promote deeper connectivity between both regions through increased passenger and cargo services. As the first such bloc-to-bloc agreement, it would be an emphatic statement of the value of multilateral cooperation in an age of disruption and fragmentation.

Friends in Need

In the post-COVID 19 world, neither ASEAN nor the EU can take our future for granted. We can do better by not taking each other for granted either. As a start, we should perhaps adhere to some simple first principles in our engagements.

First, do no harm — we should refrain from taking actions that could aggravate misunderstandings; tensions will grow and then controversy and contention will dominate the relationship.

Second, do it different — we should be bold enough to review our bottom lines and both must be willing to make compromises, and not just expect the other side to do so, the very formula that has led to deadlock.

Third, do it right — work together to co-create rules rather than accommodate the imposition of one set of standards.

Danish polymath Piet Hein defined the "The Road to Wisdom" as being to *"err and err and err again but less and less and less"*. There is a lesson in that for ASEAN-EU relations, given our past and our hopes for a better future.

Index

A

Afghanistan, 4
African, Caribbean and Pacific (ACP) countries, 4
Air France, 164
Angara, Edgardo, 126
Anglo-Malayan Defence Agreement (AMDA), 102
antimicrobial resistance (AMR), 173–174
Aquino, Benigno, 122
Arakan Army, 58
ARISE Plus Program, 70
ASEAN-10, 24
ASEAN Ad-Hoc Support Team (AHAST), 60
ASEANAPOL, 29
ASEAN-Brussels Committee (ABC), 4
ASEAN-China-EU cooperation, 97
ASEAN citizenship, 46
ASEAN Coordinating Centre for Humanitarian Assistance (AHA Centre), 59
ASEAN Defense Ministers Meeting Plus (ADMM Plus), 30, 32, 155
    Expert Working Groups (EWG), 32
    transparency and confidence building promotion, 32
ASEAN Dialogue Partners, 113
ASEAN-EC Cooperation Agreement, 4, 15, 104
ASEAN-EC Ministerial Meeting (AEMM), 4, 31
ASEAN Economic Community (AEC), 7, 14–15, 19, 21, 45, 95, 99, 113
    Blueprint 2025, 14, 114, 183
ASEAN economic integration, 21
ASEAN economy, 14
    exports and price stabilisation, 15
ASEAN-EEC Cooperation Agreement of 1980, 67
ASEAN-EU Comprehensive Air Transport Agreement (CATA), 161–162, 181, 183–184

airlines mergers, 166
direct flights, 163
fifth freedom operations and rights, 164–166
hub-to-hub operations, 162–166
single or common aviation market, 166–167
unlimited third/fourth freedom capacity, 163, 167
ASEAN-EU Free Trade Agreement (ASEAN-EU FTA), 180–181
ASEAN-EU Plan of Action, 2018–2022, 22
ASEAN-EU relations. see also strategic purpose of ASEAN-EU partnership
1972–2020, 3–8
approach of shared responsibility, 170–171
ASEAN exports to EU, 20
bilateral assistance, 19
"bloc-to-bloc" agreement, 161
capital inflow, 19
"connect the dots" approach, 181
consumer base for EU exports, 18
data regulations, 183
Digital Economy Partnership Agreement, 183
EC's share of ASEAN trade, 17
evolution of, 15–22
food security and safety, 173–174
Forest Law, Governance and Trade (FLEGT) agreements, 183
free trade agreements, 21–22, 179–184
future of, 22–25
health security, 174–176
impact of, 33
investments, 20
labour mobility, 19
manufactured exports, 16, 18
market dynamics, 162–166
merchandise trade, 16–18
Nuremberg Declaration, 170
"open skies" arrangements, 161–162
origins, 13–15
POA 2018–2022, 33
political and security cooperation, 27, 29–30, 33
strengthening of, 32–34
trade and investments, 16–20
trade development, 17, 20
values of tolerance and moderation, 54–55

ASEAN Food Safety Regulatory Framework, 174
ASEAN Free Trade Area (AFTA), 13–14
ASEAN Human Rights Declaration (AHRD), 51–52
ASEAN Intergovernmental Commission for Human Rights (AICHR), 55, 59
ASEAN Inter-Parliamentary Assembly, 40
ASEAN Investment Area (AIA), 14
ASEAN Mekong Basin Development Cooperation (AMBDC) Summit, 94
ASEAN Member States (AMS), 27, 33, 49
   right of citizens of, 54
"ASEAN minus X" formula, 41
ASEAN Plus Three, 39
ASEAN Programme for Regional Integration Support (APRIS), 6
ASEAN Regional Forum (ARF), 11, 29, 39, 104
ASEAN Regional Integration Support from the EU (ARISE), 6
ASEAN Risk Assessment Centre (ARAC), 174
Ashton, Catherine, 51
Asia-Europe Meeting (ASEM), 11, 66, 104–105
   process, 5
Asia-Invest II, 105
Asian financial crisis (AFC), 1997, 5–6, 17, 40, 87
Asian values, 51
Asia Pro Econ 11 programme, 105
Association of Southeast Asian Nations (ASEAN), 41. *See also* differences between ASEAN and EU; similarities between ASEAN and EU
   benefits to members, 45–46
   budget for annual operations of, 44–45
   Charter, 38, 40, 48
   combatting intolerance, 54
   Commission on the Rights of Women and Children, 38
   Declaration of Human Rights, 38
   dialogue partners, 27–28
   economic agreements, 40
   economic growth, 19
   external economic engagements, 45
   fight against disinformation and fake news, 52–54
   Intergovernmental Commission on Human Rights, 38
   intergovernmental organisation, 39
   peace-oriented principles, 45
   political spectrum in, 43
   response to Rohingya crisis, 57–61
   Secretariat, 47

sovereign equality in, 45
Treaty of Amity and Cooperation, 2012, 28
Australia, 14
    free trade agreements, 39

B

Bangladesh, 58
bilateral assistance, 19
bilateral dialogues, 39
Biodiversity Conservation and Management of Protected Areas in ASEAN (BCAMP), 171
Brexit, 14, 22, 25, 32, 38, 149
British nationalism, 39
Brunei Darussalam, 13, 43–45, 47
    accession into ASEAN, 69–70
    diplomatic relations with P5 members, 69
    foreign policy objectives, 69
    human rights records, 72
    vision 2035, 71
Brunei-EU relations, 72–73
    appointment of Ambassadors, 65
    cooperation in education, 66
    diplomatic ties, 65
    'donor-recipient' relationship, 70
    educational exchanges and environmental protection, 71
    overview, 65–67
    Partnership Cooperation Agreement (PCA), 66
    principle of non-interference and consensus-based decision making, 68
    priorities and interests, 67–70
    on Sharia Law Penal Code, 66, 72
    trade arrangements, 65–66
Brussels, 23, 146, 164

C

Cambodia-EU relations
    developmental cooperation, 76–77
    differences over human rights and democracy, 75

    establishment of Joint Committee (JC), 76
    Everything But Arms (EBA) preferential tariff scheme, 77, 80, 82–83
    future of, 81–84
    Multi-Annual Indicative Program (MIP), 76
    overview, 76–78
    trade arrangements, 77–78
Cambodia (Kampuchea), 4–5, 23, 41, 45–46, 51, 148
    agricultural sector, 77
    bicycle exports, 77
    economic security, 80
    economy, 77
    foreign policy, 78–80
    garment industry, 77
    Indica rice export, 77–78
    preferential access to EU market, 83
    worldview, 80
Cambodia National Rescue Party (CNRP), 77
Chan-Ocha, Prime Minister Prayut, 146, 148
chemical, biological, radiological and nuclear (CBRN) risk mitigation, 29
Chiang Mai Initiative, 40
China, 14, 24, 27, 39, 141, 148, 155
    Belt and Road Initiative (BRI), 23
    free trade agreements, 39
    investments in infrastructure, 23
Climate-ADAPT, 173
climate change, 172–173
co-funding arrangement, 67
Common Foreign and Security Policy (CFSP), 4
Communism, 17
consensus-based ASEAN member, 22
Cooperation Agreement, 15–16
Copernicus Climate Change Services, 172
Council of Europe, 60
    Commissioner for Human Rights, 61
Covid-19 global pandemic, 9, 76, 98, 141–143, 170, 174–175, 179–180, 182–184
    and global aviation industry, 168
cybercrime, 29
Cyclone Nargis, 2008, 113

D

dialogue partnerships, 27–29
differences between ASEAN and EU, 39–41
    budget, 44–45
    currency, 40
    decision-making process, 40, 43
    membership, 43–44
    Parliament, 40
    Secretariat, 40, 47
    voting, 40

E

e-ASEAN Framework Agreement, 183
East Asia Summit (EAS), 31, 39, 45
East Timor unrest, 5, 17
EC ASEAN Intellectual Property Program II (ECAP II), 105
economic impacts of trade, 23
economic integration, 37
economic liberalisation, 17
economic nationalism, 25
Eminent Persons Group (EPG), 5
Emirates Airways, 162
Enhanced Regional EU-ASEAN Dialogue Instrument (E-READI), 182
Etihad Airways, 162
EU-AICHR Policy Dialogue on Human Rights, 54
EU-ASEAN Forum on Food Safety, 2016, 174
EU Code of Practice (COP) on Disinformation, 53
euro, 40
European Coal and Steel Community (ECSC), 13, 139
European Committee of Social Rights, 61
European Community (EC), 4, 91, 104
European Convention on Human Rights
    Article 10, 52–53
European Court of Human Rights, 61
European Economic Community (EEC), 13, 65
European Environment Agency (EEA), 172
European External Action Service (EEAS), 138
European Single Market diverted trade, 17

European Union (EU), 3, 37. *See also* differences between ASEAN and EU; similarities between ASEAN and EU
  ASEAN's cooperation with, 3
  awards, 37
  budget for annual operations of, 44
  Charter of Fundamental Rights, 38
  Climate-ADAPT, 173
  climate change adaptation, 173
  combatting intolerance, 54
  "Common Position on Burma", 115
  cooperation with Cambodia, Laos, Myanmar and Vietnam (CLMV) countries, 97
  Copernicus Climate Change Services, 172
  Court of Justice of, 38
  Everything-But-Arms (EBA) trade scheme, 127
  fight against disinformation and fake news, 52–54
  Generalised Scheme of Preferences, 17
  international law and the rules-based order, 140
  'LIFE' funding programme, 172
  New Asia Strategy, 1994, 5–6
  political and economic situations, 138–139
  response to Rohingya crisis, 57–61
  restrictions against palm oil, 107
  threats to, 41
EUROPOL, 29
Eurosceptic, 139
Eurozone crisis, 22
EU SHARE programme, 171
9/11 events, 6
Everything-But-Arms (EBA) preferential trade scheme, 75
Expert Working Groups (EWG), 32

F

financial cooperation, 40
Five Power Defence Arrangement (FPDA), 102
food security and safety, 173–174
foreign direct investment (FDI), 14, 18–19
free trade agreements (FTA), 6, 14, 21–23, 38–39
  ASEAN-EU relations, 21–22, 179–184

Malaysia-EU relations, 105
Philippine-EU relations, 128–129
Singapore-EU relations, 138, 181
Thailand-EU relations, 146
Vietnam-EU relations, 150–152

G

Gabriela-Manea, Maria, 50–51
General Data Protection Regulation (GDPR), 183
Generalised Scheme of Preferences, EU, 17
Germany, 20, 149
global economic developments, 24
Global Financial Crisis 2008–09, 14, 19
globalisation, 24–25
global merchandise trade, 24–25
Greater Mekong Sub-region (GMS), 97
Green Deal, 182
Guam Doctrine, 103

H

health security, 174–176
Hein, Piet, 184
human rights
    Article 14 of Charter, 51
    ASEAN's approach towards, 38, 50–51
    "no-hate-speech" campaign, 54
Hun Sen, Prime Minister, 79, 82, 84
Hussein, Tun Abdul Razak, 103

I

India, 14, 39, 58
    free trade agreements, 39
Indonesia, 13, 20–21, 23, 41, 45–46, 50, 58–59
    defense system, 87
    environmental practices, 86
    Forest Law Enforcement, Governance and Trade (FLEGT) license, 86
    palm oil industries, 86

Indonesia-EU relations, 85
    climate change initiatives, 86–87
    comprehensive economic partnership agreement (CEPA), 88
    economic imperatives, 88
    with Germany, 87
    High Level Dialogue on Maritime and Fisheries, 88
    with Netherlands, 87
    Partnership and Cooperation Agreement (PCA), 88
    problematic issues in, 85–87
    strategic perspective, 88–89
    trust building, 89–90
international economic cooperation, 24
intolerance, 54, 142
Islamophobia, 142

J

Jakarta, 47
Japan, 14, 27, 39, 97
    free trade agreements, 39
Joint Declaration on EU-ASEAN Aviation Co-operation, 161

K

Koh, Tommy, 44
Kyi, Daw Aung San Suu, 113

L

Lancang-Mekong Cooperation (LMC), 97
Lao Lan Xang Kingdom, 91–92
Laos-EU relations, 91–92
    Cooperation Agreement of 1997, 94–96
    diplomatic relations, 91–94
    establishment of working groups (WG), 96
    EU 2014-2020 programme for Laos, 95
    EU 2016-2020 programme for Laos, 95
    Everything-But-Arms (EBA) scheme, 97–98
    recommendations for, 96–98

Socio-Economic Development Plan, 97
Laos/Lao PDR, 5, 14, 41, 43–45, 51, 75
    diplomatic relations, 91
    Eighth National Socio-Economic Development Plan (2016–2020), 95
Latin American countries, 4
Leris, G. M., 92
Leste, Timor, 37
'LIFE' funding programme, 172
Lima, Leila de, 125, 131
Lim, Jock Hoi, 47
Lopez, Ramon, 126
Lower Mekong Initiative (LMI), 97

M

Maastricht Treaty, 1991, 4
Malaysia, 13, 20–21, 23, 45–46, 50, 58–59, 85, 147, 181
    "Buy British Last" campaign, 103
    conservation efforts, 107–108
    early years of independence, 102
    Mahathir Administration 2.0, 101, 106, 108
    palm oil and palm-based products exports, 105–108
    Peace Treaty between Government and Communist Party, 102
Malaysia-EU relations, 101–102, 109
    bilateral trades, 105–108
    earlier stages, 102–104
    in economic development and trade, 103
    free trade agreement (FTA), 105
    institutionalization of, 104–105
    Partnership and Cooperation Agreement (PCA), 105
    political dialogue and economic cooperation, 105
    relations with Britain, 102–103
Malaysian Sustainable Palm Oil (MSPO) Certification Scheme, 107
Mekong-Ganga Cooperation, 97
merchandise trade, 15
Most Favoured Nation (MFN) treatment, 4, 15
Myanmar, 5, 7, 14, 17, 44, 51, 75, 148
    approach towards Rohingya population, 57–58, 61
    benfits of ASEAN membership, 116–117
    Citizenship Law, 57

relations with West, 111
Rohingya crisis, 46, 57–61, 113–115
Union Solidarity and Development Party (USDP) government, 113
Myanmar-EU relations, 111–112
    assistance for Cyclone Nargis survivors, 117
    collective approaches, 115–117
    establishing policy foundations and working mechanisms, 112–113
    EU-Myanmar Task Force, establishment of, 115
    EU's assistance for Myanmar's transition, 114–115
    human rights situation, 113
    policy of enhanced engagement, 117–119
    political-security issues, 117
    on Rohingya issue, 115, 117–118
    top investments, 116
    trade privileges, 116

N

Nargis tragedy, 117
national human rights institutions (NHRIs), 50
National Socio-Economic Development Plan (NSEDP), 95
Netherlands, 20, 149
New Zealand, 14, 183
    free trade agreements, 39
"no-hate-speech" campaign, 54
Nuclear Weapon-Free Zone, 45
Nuremberg Declaration, 170

O

Obama, President Barack, 45
old Asia strategy, 1990s, 8
Organisation for Islamic Cooperation (OIC), 59

P

Pakistan, 58
Paris Accords, 182
Parliament, 40

Philippine-EU relations, 121
  conditionalities, 125
  development aid, 127–128
  under Duterte, 121–123, 129–131
  EU grant assistance, 122
  free trade agreement (FTA) negotiations, 128–129
  future of, 129–131
  Generalised Scheme of Preferences (GSP+), 122, 125–127, 129
  non-interference, 124
  Partnership Cooperation Agreement (PCA), 122, 128
  problems, 123–126
  rapprochement by Philippines, 126–129
Philippines, 14, 20–21, 45–46, 50, 85
  anti-drug crime campaigns and extrajudicial killings, 122–123, 125
  Duterte presidency, 121–123
  Marcos dictatorship, 123
  military rule in Mindanao, 123
Phuc, Prime Minister Nguyen Xuan, 151
Portugal, 5
protectionist trade measures, 25

Q

Qatar Airways, 162

R

racism and xenophobia, 54, 142
Rahman, Tunku Abdul, 103
Rakhine State, 58–59
  ASEAN cooperation to improve conditions in, 60
Razak, Prime Minister Najib Tun, 105
Regional Comprehensive Economic Partnership (RCEP), 24, 46, 155
region-to-region trade agreement negotiations, 21, 23, 181
rights of migrant workers, 47
Rohingya crisis, 57–61, 113–115
Rohingya Muslims, 46
  repatriation and protection for, 59–60
  vulnerabilities of, 57–58
Russia, 27

S

SARS epidemic, 170
Schengen borders, 179
sea piracy, 29
Secretariat, 40
Secretary-General, 40
security problems, 169
Sein, President U Thein, 113
Senior Officials Meeting on Transnational Crimes (SOMTC), 29
similarities between ASEAN and EU, 37–39
    commitment to human rights, 38
    free trade agreements, 38
    integration of economies, 38
    labour movement, 38
    legal personalities, 37
    peace promotion, 37
Singapore, 14, 20–22, 44–46, 53, 70, 85, 183
    free trade agreements, 38
    and rivalry between China and America, 143
    trading and investment partners, 143
Singapore Airlines, 164–165
Singapore-EU relations, 137–144
    climate action and climate diplomacy, 142
    free trade agreements (FTA), 138, 181
    societal exchange and policy dialogue, 142–143
    trade and investments, 138
Singapore-Kunming Rail Link (SKRL), 93
Single Market, 14
singularity trap, 11
sixth freedom carriers, 162
Southeast Asia, 39
South Korea, 14, 39
    free trade agreements, 39
sovereignty, 39
Special Coordination Committee, 4
State of Southeast Asia, 33
strategic partnership, in ASEAN-EU relations, 4–5, 8–12, 30–31
    capacity building, 6
    "coalition of the willing" arrangements, 10
    fight against international terrorism, 6

free trade agreement (FTA), 6
market access, 4
recommendations, 11
as trading partner, 4
Suharto, President, 86
Sustainable Use of Peatland and Haze Mitigation in ASEAN (SUPA) programme, 171

T

Thailand, 14, 20–21, 41, 45–46, 50, 53, 58, 85, 181
    fishing industry, 145–146
    military junta, 145–146
Thailand-EU relations, 145–148
    anti-illegal, unregulated, and unreported (IUU) fishing, 148
    bilateral free trade agreement, 146
    human rights and developmental approaches, 147
    Partnership and Cooperation Agreement, 148
Timor-Leste, 37, 44, 45*fn*
trade liberalisation, impact of, 16
trade relations, for ASEAN countries, 16–20
Trans-Pacific Partnership (TPP), 24
Trans-Regional EU-ASEAN Trade Initiative, 2003, 18
Treaty of Amity and Cooperation in Southeast Asia (TAC), 1976, 45, 124
Trump, President Donald, 25, 148
Turkish Airlines, 162
Tusk, Donald, 148

U

UK, 4, 20, 149
UK Permanent Mission, 24
United Nations (UN), 11
    Convention on the Law of the Sea, 40
    Declaration of Human Rights, 51
    General Assembly, 59
    Human Rights Council (HRC), 123
    Special Rapporteur on Extrajudicial Killings, 130
Universal Periodic Review (UPR) process, 55
US, 27, 39, 97, 148
US-China strategic rivalry, 33

V

Vietnam, 14, 20–22, 41, 43, 45, 51, 53, 75, 85
Vietnam Chamber of Commerce and Industry (VCCI), 152
Vietnam-EU relations, 149–157
    bilateral economic relations, 150–152
    Cooperation Agreement, 150
    defence cooperation, 154–155
    Framework Participation Agreement (FPA), 155
    free trade agreement (EVFTA), 150–152
    Investment Protection Agreement (EVIPA), 151
    problems, 153–154
    rules-based order, 154–156

W

Wong, Reuben, 152
Wuysthoff, Gerrot Van, 92

X

Xi, Jinping, President, 83

www.ingramcontent.com/pod-product-compliance
Lightning Source LLC
Chambersburg PA
CBHW072043160426
43197CB00014B/2608